HERBERT HOOVER'S HIDEAWAY

The Story of Camp Hoover on the Rapidan River

in

Shenandoah National Park

by

DARWIN LAMBERT

1971
Bulletin No. 4
SHENANDOAH NATURAL HISTORY ASSOCIATION, Inc.
Luray, Virginia 22835

Published In Cooperation with:
THE NATIONAL PARK SERVICE,
U. S. DEPARTMENT OF THE INTERIOR.

Reprinted 1983

President Herbert Hoover. (Underwood & Underwood, Library of Congress)

PREFACE

by JOEL T. BOONE

White House Physician to Presidents Harding, Coolidge and Hoover.

It was not very long after President Hoover was inaugurated into Presidential office on March 4, 1929, that he realized that he must find release at suitable intervals from the confinement of a most demanding office which administered in general, and in great detail in many instances, the governmental institutions of the United States of America. Pressure on him from the day of his assuming that office and throughout his four years' directing it, with international involvements such as our country heretofore had never experienced, was recognized by him as such that he would have to have restful release from time to time. With his extensive contacts in many parts of the world, he brought into his Presidential office a greatly broader base and a familiarity in general with the operation of many foreign governments such as the United States Presidents had never theretofore experienced.

He and his highly intelligent and wonderful wife were devotees of the great outdoors, wanting to be closely a part of it. They had traveled and lived in many parts of the world and knew, that with all the challenges of his office and subjected to constant pounding of activity and the heaviest kind of omnipresent pressures, he must find a place, not too far away from Washington, where he could relax and enjoy in as much quietude as possible the blessings of nature.

He had always liked sports of various types, but I believe his most favorite one was fishing, in which he participated wherever he found facilities to do so and as frequently as possible. He found by doing so that he could be respirited and relaxed when he was alone fishing in streams or large bodies of water. When he was fishing in streams he wanted to be entirely alone. He said, after he assumed the highest of offices, that fish had no respect for personages, of whatever status, that "Fishing is a constant reminder of the democracy of life, of humility and of human frailty—for all men are equal before fishes," and that "everybody considers that fish will not bite in the presence of the public." He thought it was a sport that made for humility, which was a blessing for the head of a nation to experience; however, Herbert Hoover was by nature a modest and unassuming and, to a considerable extent, a shy man. He never thought any effort he made to turn his hand in service to his country or his fellowman was beneath his dignity.

Before setting forth to look for some place to provide him with recreation and rest, he talked to many people, no doubt, but most with Mrs. Hoover. He studied some maps and made certain surveys of areas, besides having others do it for him. He wanted a place not too far from Washington and which was readily accessible to the nation's capital. He conceived the idea that 100 miles distance from Washington would be the proper limits for him to select for such a place. He wanted streams; he wanted to establish a rustic camp off the mainstream of traffic; he wanted woodland, views of mountains, and well set apart from the so-called beaten path.

One Saturday in the spring of 1929 he and Mrs. Hoover decided to set forth toward the area of Shenandoah National Park. President and Mrs. Hoover took with them his senior Naval Aide, Captain Wilson Brown; Larry Richey, one of his secretaries who well knew the out-of-doors; Secretary of the Interior Ray Lyman Wilbur, another who loved the great out-of-doors and knew it well; Major Earl C. Long, U. S. Marine Corps, who was a Californian and graduate in civil engineering of the University of California; and myself as his physician. Mounting horses lent by people of Madison County at the foot of the Blue Ridge Mountain of Virginia, we climbed a rugged mountain trail and thence into a valley where there was a beautiful stream. The horses traveled the stream bed until we found a place that impressed the President as ideal for his requirements; so a camp was selected and then subsequently established with the cabin to be built for President and Mrs. Hoover at the focal point of the camp, which expanded into a sizable recreational institution. Its use in time proved its justification to be made into a shrine bearing Herbert Hoover's name, that all visitors seeing it could hopefully take in some of the inspiring atmosphere that it created when established and throughout its existence as a camp. It has become a shrine and exhibit in the Shenandoah National Park. At this camp was centered significant portions of the story of President and Mrs. Hoover as individuals briefly escaping the spotlight's glare and living in communion with the American earth while continuing to serve the people of the country and all humanity. From the splendid streams, forests and mountains, both of the Hoovers drew strength and inspiration for their public service, and in turn their strong personalities permeated the camp and moved out into projects of conservation, wise development, and helpfulness to their neighbors of the Blue Ridge and the Piedmont country.

The relevance of President Hoover's life to current conditions is widely recognized, and books about it continue to appear. Only in this present volume, however, do readers find the public and private stories as lived at this refuge in the wilderness deeply traced and revealed in their interweavings.

As President Hoover's personal physician, which was encompassed in the legal title, "The Physician to the White House," I was at the camp whenever he was for the four years of his Presidency, so I believe I am able to confirm the authenticity and understanding which marked this telling, at least, of the combined story. Written materials, both published and unpublished were utilized; but the book for which this writing is the preface, and living detail come largely from interviews with persons who knew the camp and the Hoovers during his Presidential years and from the author's familiarity with this section of the Blue Ridge.

Guests who were invited to the camp accepted the invitations with alacrity after hearing of its uniqueness and charm. The President, while he did not use it for a workshop, found occasions when he invited a wide gamut of guests: governors, bankers, legislators, industrialists, educators, scientists, authors, members of the legal profession, physicians, researchers of various types, government officials, including military, etc., etc. There were other times when he brought members of commissions, that he had appointed on various projects, who conferred jointly from time to time with him and he with them, but, as his physician, I was always happy when he had more relaxed personal friends than public officials and industrialists, bankers, geologists, etc., because when he did have the latter, he would become very absorbed and in concentrating on the business at hand was prevented from getting the recreation and rest that he needed. It seemed to me that during his Presidential administration there was always something "blowing up in the President's face." His was certainly a very strenuous four-year Presidency. It seemed that he always was compelled to be fighting battles, strikes of one sort or another, unusual financial problems and broad-scale emergencies.

One of the most productive enterprises that President and Mrs. Hoover conceived was the building and establishment of a school for mountain children, which became really a community center. I have always been inexpressibly gratified that I located, by a chance meeting, Ray Buracker, the little mountaineer boy. With the President, through me, baiting him to come to the President's camp where he met President and Mrs. Hoover from which contact the mountain school resulted. Fortunately, the mountaineer teacher acquired from Kentucky was Miss Christine Vest, who had been educated at Berea College. She was truly a most valuable find, for she supervised the school and the community center and rightly deserved the credit. It became a broadly expanded institution of education and community development for mountaineer children and their elders. It seemed to bring the Blue Ridge Mountains of Virginia from a nebulous, local beginning into a wide spectrum of creative and constructive influence in a wide area of the Virginia mountains, broadening out from a core which was the Hoover Camp.

Preface is not a place, I realize, to be expansive in literary pursuit. The President's Rapidan Camp, its activities, and the many human beings who have benefited from its existence, opened a new vista of learning and an entrance into a larger world than a mountain fastness ordinarily could have provided.

The history of the Rapidan Camp has been well recorded, and all pertaining thereto in people and activities has been well documented. Its contribution to the health of Herbert Hoover as president of the United States, Mrs. Hoover, their children, and a wide gamut of friends and acquaintances can obviously be visualized as important to the maintenance of unusually good health on the part of the Principals. The Camp made it possible, I feel as a physician, for President and Mrs. Hoover to come through a very arduous four-year Presidential administration period without any serious physical impairments. Without the Rapidan Camp, now more specifically referred to as the Hoover Camp, President and Mrs. Hoover could hardly have left official life without any serious ailments. The author of the book for which this Preface is provided has so well stated: "Human interest is found here in rich abundance, added to the meaning of Camp Hoover in the working out of conservation as a significant ingredient of the American way of life, and to the other major threads which make up the coloration and poignant fabric of history."

I cannot conclude the preparation of this Preface without the thought expressed that my own life has been enriched in countless ways due to the privileged and intimate relationships I had with Camp Hoover from the day the geographical area was located, selected, and thence built up to fashion Camp Hoover until it ceased to exist under the ownership of President Hoover. He provided it for the use, as desired, of his Presidential successors, and with it ultimately being presented to the Shenandoah National Park.

JOEL T. BOONE
Vice Admiral, Medical Corps, U. S. Navy
Retired

TABLE OF CONTENTS

I

Fountain Of Youth

Persons who knew Camp Hoover have been coming back. They walk over the grounds and along the streams and look into the remaining buildings — and remember. Some of them who have served around the world have come back to Virginia to live. There is stronger than normal cohesion among those who knew the Hoovers well, perhaps especially among those who remember when "the Chief" and "the Lady" — as they were fondly called — came frequently to the Rapidan. Correspondence is still exchanged, and when they get together there are reminiscences.

They share gladly with others who show interest, and they feel that Camp Hoover should not be forgotten. Some of them have volunteered to help record the story, believing that if it is written the people of today will treasure the camp and perhaps will come to receive meaningful messages from the not-so-long-ago past. Long reminiscences have been caught on tape, others in scribbled notes. Files have been searched. Published materials, mostly newspapers, have been studied. The savings of many memories have been gathered.

The story began after the votes had been counted in November 1928 and Herbert Hoover knew the American people wanted him, not Al Smith, as President. Long before he took office (inauguration was not until March 4 then) the pressures that would become almost unbearable during four years of insecurity and depression began zeroing in on him. He knew he would need to get away at intervals from the intensifying tempo — what he had already labeled the "pneumatic hammer" of persons and problems constantly jolting high public office — and renew his strength and balance in more restful surroundings.

Being more fully conscious than most men of basic sources of renewal, he gave Lawrence Richey, perhaps his most intimate secretary, this assignment: Find a summer-camp site on a trout stream within 100 miles of Washington, at an elevation of 2500 feet or more so as to be away from mosquito-breeding waters and have a climate affording relief from the capital city's exhausting heat (no air-conditioning in those days).

Richey was the right man for this apparently simple but actually complex and significant task. An outdoorsman himself, he knew trout streams and camp sites. He also knew the Hoovers — the engineer-turned statesman, Lou Henry Hoover, who had ideas of her own, and the two sons — which was even more important. He had been in the Chief's corner during many hard-fought bouts, beginning when Hoover headed the U. S. Food Administration after this country entered World War I, continuing through Hoover's chairmanship of the food section of the Allied Supreme Economic Council, of the American Relief Administration and the European Relief Council, and through the two terms as Secretary of Commerce. Now he was with Hoover in facing the Presidency.

Richey remembered Hoover's words explaining why the Germans should be fed: "We do not kick a man in the stomach after we have licked him... We have not been fighting women and children and we are not beginning now... Our vision must stretch over the next hundred years, and we must write now into history such acts as will stand creditably in the minds of our grandchildren." A battler who refused defeat even when Congress rejected funds for feeding enemy countries, who took the fight to the American people and persuaded them to contribute millions of dollars for feeding German children and nursing mothers, was truly special to Richey, deserving the best of all possible places to relax.

So — what type of fishing camp? What degree of isolation? What kind of neighbor, if any? And where indeed within 100 miles of Washington would there not be neighbors? Perhaps, then, neighbors who, instead of hammering on nerves already sore from Presidential pressures, would be a distracting element. People isolated from the demanding crises of the nation and the world? People who might even increase the Chief's temporary distance from official duties by involving the personal understanding which was so ingrained in the Hoover character?

Richey has not lived to return to Camp Hoover in the nineteen-sixties, and his mind can be explored only through others and through files that remain available. Clearly, however, he considered the whole complicated nature and background of the Chief in facing the camp-finding assignment.

Quaker parents had brought Herbert Hoover into a world of woods and streams and productive soil in eastern Iowa. The

Lawrence Richey (left) with Dr. Joel T. Boone, putting together
a jigsaw puzzle on Camp Hoover grounds.

Chief had often recalled, with Richey and others, the old
swimming hole hidden in willows near an Iowa bridge, and
Cook's Hill where he coasted on a homemade sled — and angl-
ing for sunfish, catfish and suckers with a willow pole and a
worm on a one-cent hook, and live-trapping rabbits with the
aid of a figure-4 trigger.

Richey knew the grown-up Hoover's response to the
question of what subjects he had most enjoyed in grade school:
"None of them. They were all something to race through so I
could get out of doors." Richey knew of the early death of
both parents and of the period of financial hardship, of the
years with a relative in Oregon when the youth found the
consolation of outdoor life in surroundings very different from
Iowa. He knew, too, of the extensive early reading — Scott,
Thackeray and Dickens, then Shakespeare, then history with
emphasis on American pioneering and the blossoming of prosperity from individual self-reliance in cooperation with nature,
— studies and campus leadership at Stanford contemporary

with that California university's beginnings, and of the spectacular successes as a mining engineer in California, Australia, China, and elsewhere around the planet.

Richey's extraordinary loyalty grew partly from admiration of the Chief's dramatic shift from lucrative eminence as a mining engineer to donated leadership of a quickly formed organization that brought 150,000 Americans safely out of Europe when war caught them, followed by another informal organization that overcame monstrous obstacles to supply food and clothing to millions of civilians in war-devastated areas such as Belgium. It was such volunteer initiative that led to Hoover's more formal position with the Allies and the U. S. Government and his final refusal to resume his profession even when the Guggenheims offered a wealth-producing partnership in the world's largest mining and metallurgical firm. In words apparently used first by another of Hoover's friends, Will Irwin, the Chief as Secretary of Commerce had graduated to "engineering our material civilization as a whole — without goose-stepping the human spirit or blueprinting the human soul" — and wanted to carry the same work farther as President.

Richey considered Mrs. Hoover also in searching for the ideal campsite, knowing that if she did not find pleasure there the Chief would not. Lou Henry was a Stanford graduate too, having insisted on delaying her marriage until she could complete her major in geology, even if the delay did necessitate Hoover's returning from far-away Australia to claim her. She shared nearly all her husband's interests, including his taste for the out-of-doors — but in her own individual ways. "One of the ablest women we ever had at Stanford," said an executive of that university. Shortly after coming to live in Washington she had become president of the Girl Scouts of America, and at the time of Richey's search she was far along in building that organization into a powerful force for good, adding more than two million dollars to its coffers, multiplying its enrollment tenfold to almost a million girls.

The whole family, in fact, was both nature-oriented and people-oriented. During the Secretary-of-Commerce years, Mrs. Hoover added a porch at the back of their house and developed a splendid garden — much of it "woodsy" with forest flowers and trees, a small pond, a path or two. Summer meals were frequently eaten outdoors. The Chief often called

4

the attention of guests, including Richey, to the bright flowers, and he gloried in the great oaks which had survived from the primeval forest.

Younger son Allan was especially fond of animals, insisting a family of four needed two dogs and two cats at the very least. He put gourds in trees as nesting sites and was lavish with food and water to keep birds about. He acquired two ducks which he trained to sit on the front porch, amusing neighbors and passersby. He accumulated turtles, fortunately land, not water types. Only when someone gave him two alligators, and he decided their proper place was in the bathtubs, did other members of the family rebel.

The Hoovers lived or camped in many of the world's scenic places, and Richey knew that just any good trout stream at 2500 feet would not satisfy. They needed inspirational scenery and, if possible, a complete natural environment. Hoover and sons had taken to the trees at one rural retreat, building a tree-house and, incidentally, attracting numerous helpers (a la Tom Sawyer). At another place Hoover had exercised his engineering ability in lifting back into place and permanently supporting a storm-cracked, tons-heavy branch of a huge oak tree.

Hoover's friends had long recognized that much of his remarkable strength and endurance came from contact with the natural earth, and they often spoke of how, even in Europe, he would take his family and others into the countryside, stop at some spot of maximum seclusion, build a small fire, and treat the party to bacon and eggs. Then he would relax directly on the ground, perhaps leaning on a tree trunk.

But Richey knew, partly through being a fisherman himself that the strength of earth was likely to flow most strongly into the Chief while fishing. Shortly after being made an honorary member of the Izaak Walton League, Hoover had addressed a League session in such words as these:

> Man and boy, the American is a fisherman. That comprehensive list of human rights, the Declaration of Independence, is firm that all men (and boys) are endowed with certain inalienable rights, including life, liberty, and the pursuit of happiness, which obviously includes the pursuit of fish...
>
> The fishing beatitudes are much amplified since Izaak Walton, for he did not spend his major life answering a bell. He never got the jumps from traffic signals or the price of

wheat. The blessings of fishing include not only Edgar Guest's "wash of the soul" with pure air, but they also now include discipline in the equality of men, meekness and inspiration before the works of nature, charity and patience toward tackle makers and the fish, a mockery of profits and conceits, a quieting of hate and a hushing of ambition, a rejoicing and gladness that you do not have to decide a darned thing until next week...

No other organized joy has values comparable to the outdoor experience. We gain less from the other forms in moral stature, in renewed purpose in life, in kindness, and in all the fishing beatitudes. We gain none of the constructive rejuvenating joy that comes from return to the solemnity, the calm and inspiration of primitive nature. The joyous rush of the brook, the contemplation of the eternal flow of the stream, the stretch of forest and mountain all reduce our egotism, soothe our troubles, and shame our wickedness. And in it we make a physical effort that no sitting on cushions, benches, or sidelines provides...

The Chief declared further, sometimes, that "fishing is the eternal fountain of youth," and went on to describe a tablet allegedly engraved in the year 2,000 B.C., stating, "The gods do not subtract from the allotted span of men's lives the hours spent in fishing."

A "fountain of youth" — yes. Lawrence Richey had been given an assignment that meant much to Herbert Hoover, would even influence the Presidency, so it meant much to him also. He obtained maps and plotted curves on them representing the 100-mile distance from Washington. He noted the limited number of places where elevations rose to 2500 feet. Then he wrote postmasters for meaningful facts about their communities and surroundings. Winter had come now, and the campsite search was only one of his innumerable tasks in helping Hoover prepare for the Presidential term, but even so he began reconnoitering the more promising areas. He stopped to ask questions or merely to listen while having coffee or a meal in roadside restaurants where those who knew the land might gather. He explored remote roads until they became impassable in snow or mud, boulders or briers. Sometimes he hired horses or even took to shoe leather, determined to leave no spot unexamined which might best serve.

Word of the search spread, and a news flurry clouded

the plan in mid-December. Congressman Woodrum of Virginia (possibly urged by retiring President Calvin Coolidge) introduced a joint resolution calling upon the Public Buildings Commission to collect data regarding places that might be available for a "summer White House," then to conduct hearings and make recommendations. Accompanied by Congressman Elliott of Indiana, chairman of the House public buildings committee, Woodrum called upon Coolidge, who had less than three months of his term left, to discuss the matter.

Coolidge said he favored not a permanent summer home but merely a place accessible to the capital city where Presidents might spend the night or a weekend. He suggested that Weather Bureau property in the Blue Ridge Mountains near Bluemont, Virginia, might serve — with an expenditure of,say, $25,000 to make it livable. It was learned and publicly announced that sites in Maryland and Pennsylvania had been proposed also to congressmen.

Rising to competition, the Berryville (Virginia) Chamber of Commerce immediately urged Congress to provide a summer White House at the Mt. Weather site. The chamber resolution pointed to the 80-acre government-owned tract "which overlooks Shenandoah River and could easily be converted into a home for the Presidents' rest and recreation — high, healthful, secluded and accessible to good fishing and bridle paths." This Weather Bureau property was 60 miles from Washington over a state highway.

Harold Allen, a Washington attorney who had in 1924 been first to suggest that the proposed Shenandoah National Park be created around the Skyland resort, saw the news accounts and promptly advised friends in Virginia to propose Skyland and Stony Man Mountain. A telegram was sent by park booster L. Ferdinand Zerkel of Luray to Senator Claude A. Swanson, urging a site in either the Skyland or Thornton Gap sector, claiming both easy accessibility and opportunity for total seclusion.

To what extent, if at all, Hoover and Richey were influenced by this public flurry is unknown, but clearly they were not leaving the decision to a committee or commission, to Coolidge or Congress. Along the eastern edge of the Virginia Blue Ridge, especially where Stony Man and Hawksbill reach elevations above 4,000 feet, people noticed, however, more and

more often the comings and goings of a quiet stranger — who might, some of them thought, be a revenue officer in search of moonshine stills.

He was seen one warmish winter day in the county-seat town of Madison. Out in front of Hunton Inn stood an old lamp, a dinner bell, and split-bottom chairs. Oldtimers of the district including John T. Hall of the Inn, known as the sheriff who did not carry a gun, had a habit of gathering there for talk. The stranger leaned back in one of those chairs, made friendly comments about the weather, and waited. Everyone was careful not to mention moonshine, but somehow the talk turned to fishing. Perhaps the stranger said the day felt like the opening of fishing season. At any rate, the oldtimers were soon telling of trout they had caught in the Rapidan and Robinson (Robertson) rivers. The stranger listened intently and after a while went on his way, perhaps to listen at another gathering up or down the Ridge.

On January 27, 1929, Mrs. Hoover sent a long letter to a close friend, revealing progress for which Richey was largely responsible:

> I can't believe it is a week today since we went roaming off into the country to look at possible campsites... We looked over some miles of a fair fishing stream ... and a goodly number of sites presented themselves, all of value chiefly because they are such a short distance from Washington, not quite two and a half hours on a good motor road...
>
> The country we saw was mostly gently sloping mountain land rising 2500 or 3000 feet, with some picturesque bold outlines... Excepting where occasional benches have been cleared for corn or a few old orchards by the primitive mountain folk, the slopes are very well wooded with a youngish growth. There are innumerable, enormous dead chestnuts standing all over the place, so that it must have been a very different place after the foliage was out a dozen years ago. Also

Ghost Chestnut Trees killed by blight before the Hoovers came. (NPS)

along the streams and hillside that we covered were many very large bare trees, mostly felled over a dozen or twenty years ago. We were told that they had been brought down only for their bark, not even the lumber being utilized! Which seems perfectly wicked!...

We discussed the proposed camp as we explored... Much the same problems might be involved as with certain Girl Scout camps, the more substantial features expected to last from summer to summer. The vital parts might be possible of occupancy during late autumn and early spring, or even for an occasional snow camp.

It seems to me that good board flooring and a roof, with a boarded strip extending up perhaps three feet from the floor and with or without a similar strip below the eaves, with the sides composed of canvas curtains that let up and down as weather dictates, might answer this year's needs for the eating and congregating centers — not unlike some of the Girl Scout mess halls, and like some of the camps in your East, and in our

Sierras where we must meet occasional rain and cold.

There would need to be two or three picturesque sturdy shacks entirely of wood and with very substantial underpinnings, for food storehouse and office supplies, whose contents won't blow away even with the gales that those mountains have occasionally.

Sleeping quarters might be of much the same construction as the mess and living quarters, but in smaller units. One would wake up to the feeling that he was on a sleeping porch, and yet part of it would be securely enough anchored to the earth not to blow away or get the contents wet. Incidentally, some opening could be left wide enough that a bed could be pulled straight out on a platform under the stars without much ado, and could be as hastily pushed back under cover when the first sprinkle came.

Conditions necessitate a rather biggish establishment. There must be room for 18 or 20 people to eat, with a feeling of spaciousness — architecturally not gastronomically. And for the same number to sit in another portion of the same structure, probably the two to open into each other, or to be a part of the same "room," to help with this feeling of spaciousness. And naturally it must have a field-stone fireplace! Even if it is only used one season!

My husband's and my quarters would have to include a bathroom...sleeping quarters...a couple of dressing rooms, one perhaps involved in the wet weather sleeping room. Whether he wants a study or work room connected with his sleeping quarters or whether the one connected with his office will be sufficient for him, I do not know. But certainly connected with, or within a very short dash of it, I would want a work room of my own that would be picturesque enough to be used as my sitting room, and yet isolated enough for me to leave my work scattered around without any compunctions about my tidying it up!

There would need to be three or four units of guest rooms, perhaps each unit with two or three or four sleeping, and dressing rooms, connected with half as many bathrooms and some kind of a mutual lounging place, perhaps some of the latter enclosed and some not.

In another building must be some offices where the men may work and two or three secretaries have their separate diggings, with a biggish room for as many stenographers and typewriters... Then there would have to be quarters for cooks,

Mrs. Herbert Hoover (Underwood & Underwood, Library of Congress)

and servants enough to take care of all these people, chauffeurs to come and go, some protection for cars out of the weather; and room for at least a half-dozen Secret Service men — and very likely a small detachment of Uncle Sam's Army or Marine Corps! These latter units must be quite out of sight of the main camp and yet close enough that their men on duty could get back and forth easily...

My husband's idea was to have a camp down on one of the tree-covered flats beside a stream or at the junction between two streams. He likes to be near enough to hear the water murmuring. A spot might be found where part of the camp could be down there and part of it a hundred or so feet higher on one of the broad benches giving a distant view...

At the end of that time we were met by a Shenandoah Park official who knows the entire neighborhood for a hundred miles around. He told us that a dozen miles farther south, but on another road and an equal driving distance from Washington, was a stream infinitely better for fishing and infinitely more picturesque than the one we saw, with 18 miles of uninhabited length to choose a site from. It was too late for us to go the roundabout road to get from where we were to this other stream, and we were leaving for the Florida trip early the next morning. But it was decided then that some spot on this other stream would be selected for a comparatively temporary camp for this summer, and that during the early stages of its occupation everyone would probably be exploring around until someone hit upon the ideal place for a more or less permanent camp...

The "Shenandoah Park official" was William E. Carson, chairman of the Virginia State Conservation and Development Commission. Though Carson, like Richey, is gone, the Hoover Presidential Library at West Branch, Iowa, has many communications they exchanged. Carson was then engaged in the vast task of raising funds and buying hundreds of thousands of acres to be presented to the Federal government for the national park. He thus had a complex jigsaw puzzle to put together — and already, behind the scenes, for a time even farther behind them than Richey, he was preparing to use the Hoover hideaway in shaping the picture.

The grapevine carried different accounts of how Carson became involved. It was said he got wind of the search through the postmaster at Criglersville, who had received one of Richey's first letters of inquiry, and that he went to see Hoover (with whom he had become acquainted during the war) and sold him on the Rapidan River. This is an extreme simplification, for between Carson's learning of the search and the granting of approval to the Rapidan location came amazing maneuvers. The enterprising Virginian had borrowed the ball and was running with it while communicating with Richey in Washington and the Hoovers in Florida. By letter of February 25 Carson told Hoover:

> All the fishing rights have been secured in my name and are so recorded in the land records of Madison County.
>
> The stocking of the streams is in the hands of the proper persons and is being attended to... I am having the stream patrolled to keep off poachers.
>
> An appropriation has been jointly made by the state highway department and the county of Madison to put a road from the state highway into the Rapidan basin in good travelable shape.
>
> When you are satisfied the stream is what you want in quality, seclusion, remoteness and accessibility, and choose a camp site, *I will have a suitable camp built.*
>
> There has been no newspaper publicity on this matter and won't be if I can keep it down.

On the last point he was underestimating W. D. Bushong of the Madison County *Eagle* who caught up with the situation on March 1 under this headline, "Madison County May Get Summer White House": Tom T. Early, an avid local fisherman employed by the national park branch of the state conservation commission, had told his boss (Carson) of the excellent fishing on the Rapidan. Soon thereafter Carson began visiting landowners. He quickly secured fishing-right options covering 10,000 acres, then invited Madison leaders to a big dinner at Hunton Inn. After they were well fed, he confided his scheme. The fishing rights, he declared, brought it within reach, but a tremendous effort was still necessary. Minimum additional needs included a new road (then estimated at 6.7 miles from Criglersville into the upper Rapidan) and a direct phone line to Washington from the remote site. Before leaving Hunton Inn, the county supervisors, led by E. E. Chapman, promised $7,000 (plus $2,500 if needed) to start road construction (state aid expected to come later). Within a very few days the Chesapeake & Potomac Telephone Co. agreed to spend $100,000 for the phone line.

The *Eagle* commented that hope hinged on (1) Madison County's having "gone for" Hoover in November's election, (2) the fine fishing (altruistically sacrificed by the Rapidan Fishing Club which would probably move to the Robinson River), and (3) fast action on the road and other such needs as they became known.

The secret was out. News reporters began converging on Madison. The situation developed so swiftly now, along so many lines, both behind the curtain and in front of it, that no one man could keep track of it all, though Richey, Carson, and Major Earl C. Long (a U. S. Marine Corps engineer who had unobtrusively taken a room at Hunton Inn) came close. Tom Early and others guided Richey and Long around the Rapidan watershed, using old cars as far as they could go, then horses and, in places human footwork. Airplanes were ultimately called in to help fit the ground observations into the over-all puzzle.

The *Eagle* of March 22 headlined, "Upper Rapidan Officially Chosen as Fishing Lodge for President Hoover," and related how, the previous Saturday, Carson, Richey, Horace M. Albright (director, National Park Service), Henry O'Malley (U. S. Commissioner of Fisheries), J. H. Albright (district engineer, Virginia highway department), and others had gathered for a meal at Hunton Inn, then proceeded to the preserve leased by Carson. A Col. Price of the highway department, who had ridden horseback separately over a different route, gave them his ideas of where and how the needed road could be built in record time. Upon returning from that excursion, Richey (as personal representative of the President) accepted the upper Rapidan, with the probability of a lodge being constructed on the "Wilhoite place," O'Malley said he would arrange to have the Rapidan stocked with fish from Federal sources — though Carson had already solved that "problem" through state facilities and Madison guides declared the stream to be already "full of brook, brown and rainbow trout," having been well managed by the Rapidan Fishing Club which had acquiesced in transfer of rights to Carson for Hoover (partly in consideration of a state promise to augment stocking of nearby Robinson, or Robertson, River). Redundance of fish in the Rapidan seemed likely.

Horace Albright recently recalled that excursion, the splendid horse he rode (lent by a local lady), and the hours spent exploring. Then: "We were about to go back, and everybody was happy, particularly Mr. Carson and the local people who were with us, when I raised the question of rattlesnakes. I said, 'Is there any chance of that valley up there having rattlesnakes?' Well, that just threw the whole thing into commotion, don't you know. We had to find out about that!

"Two families were homesteaders there...so we rapidly constituted a committee of Bill Starling (head of the Secret Service) and myself to interview these people about rattlesnakes. Both families told us there were very few rattlesnakes — they thought because they had razorback hogs loose in the valley... But you know none of us thought about copperheads. And so when the camp was being built they found a lot of copperheads in several different parts of it."

(Among facts he did not disclose was that Congressman-elect J. A. Garber, while not ruling out other streams in his district, had been an advocate of the Hughes. Garber had lagged behind Carson — but not far. In a March 14 letter to Richey he had revealed he had a man ready to secure Hughes River fishing options but had held off pending actual decision by Hoover.) The *Eagle* gleefully hailed the Rapidan's victory — not so much over Hughes River as over the Mt. Weather "summer White House" for which Congress had appropriated $48,000 in an expansion upon Coolidge's suggestion.

On March 25 Carson mailed to Richey "a full set of plans for the proposed fishing lodge... When you O.K. these plans, we will commence to assemble the material... Won't you please have ... the President ... make any suggestions for correction or improvement?" This ambitious Virginia scheme to create a $100,000 Presidential fishing camp as a gift, largely to further the proposed Shenandoah National Park, was successfully withheld from the press.

But the *Eagle* eye remained reasonably sharp and reported on March 29 that the Rapidan access road was not only under contract already but actually under construction, and that Madison Power Company had started an extension of its electric line from Criglersville toward the Wilhoite place.

There remained, however, amid all the eager and confusing action, the possibly crucial matter of showing the proposed site and plans to the Hoovers themselves. Much as Hoover was known to trust Richey, the two could not always see exactly alike — or could they? And did Richey actually approve the Virginia gift idea, much as he appreciated the farflung organizational work done by Carson?

President Hoover riding near the camp. (Library of Congress)

The inauguration had now taken place, and Hoover excursions could no longer be spur-of-the-moment affairs. Advance arrangements were made with great care. Among other details, Mrs. Hoover was to change into her riding habit at Hunton Inn. Several hours before the White House party was due, Secret Service personnel entered the inn and began, according to local memories, clearing out the people, many of them overnight guests or residents of the establishment, some only half through their breakfast. Mrs. Wade Blankenbaker, in charge of the inn at the time, protested.

"But we have made arrangements," the leader of the SS group said.

"Not this kind of arrangements. These people belong here, and they wouldn't bother Mrs. Hoover anyway."

"But we must clear the place out and search —"

Mrs. Blankenbaker stopped the SS man with a glare. "If this is true," she said, "you will simply have to make other arrangements."

The oral versions go on to tell how the people remained, protected against the Secret Service by the indomitable Mrs. Blankenbaker, how the Hoovers arrived as scheduled, and the people paid no more attention to them than they would have to any other arrivals (thus demonstrating the Madison brand of sophistication).

The *Eagle*, however, reporting the Hoovers' first inspection of the Rapidan, stated that, while a brief stop was made at Hunton Inn, the change to riding habit was at the E. E. Chapman home in Criglersville where the big cars from the White House were parked and Model A Fords taken. Where wilderness halted the Fords (furnished free by a dealer in Washington) horses were substituted (lent free by Madison County citizens). The paper pointedly mentioned Charles Y. Rippin, an architect and personal friend of Hoover, as being along — perhaps to check over the Virginia plans? perhaps to help draw different plans?

Fork Mountain and Hoover country from Hoover schoolhouse site. (NPS)

A local horseman-guide told of a stroke of fear that the whole idea would be abandoned. He overheard the Hoovers, he said, expressing dissatisfaction with the Wilhoite site. But then, as the party climbed farther upriver, he observed the Hoover enthusiasm growing, and his confidence returned.

Joel T. Boone (Vice Admiral, M.C., U. S. Navy, Retired) who, as the President's personal physician, was with him on every visit to the Rapidan, a distinction that not even Mrs. Hoover or Richey could claim, remembers vivid details. Boone said the horseback party — also including Secretary of the Interior Ray Lyman Wilbur, Richey, Maj. Long, Carson, and Presidential naval aide Capt. Brown — rode over Chapman Mountain and down to the river. They then rode upstream, often splashing right in the water on gravel and boulders, the "rough fishing trails" seldom being adequate for horses. The President — "who loathed riding, though Mrs. Hoover liked it" — dismounted after a time. He walked up and down the river and its branches, looking and listening. He liked the appearance of the place and the sounds of the water. After a time he pointed to the somewhat level land between Mill and Laurel prongs, where they join to form the river, and said, "That's where I want my camp."

The *Eagle* bannered its front page of April 12:
"HOOVER VISITS AND ACCEPTS!"

II

Instant Village

To an observer not equipped to watch and interpret the swiftly spreading preparations, Camp Hoover appeared like spring mushrooms (the "mirkles" or "miracles" of the mountain folk). Even to most of the insiders the process was semi-magical as though, once set going, it automatically and almost instantly bore fruit.

The Hoovers' architect-friend, even before the weekly *Eagle* had time to announce the President's approval, addressed to Richey and Maj. Long a letter detailing facilities to be provided. It corresponded to ideas expressed in Mrs. Hoover's January letter, which had survived a Hoover-Richey-Rippin conference on April 8, and called for ten tents. One was to be 20 by 20 feet and nine to be 14 by 14, all placed on wooden frames with floors a foot above ground and board sidewalls rising five feet. There would also be an all-frame dining room-kitchen. Two tents intended for use by the Hoovers themselves would have field-stone chimneys and fireplaces.

Carson and company, meanwhile, kept moving aggressively forward, still expecting to construct a luxurious Presidential lodge with funds provided by the Commonwealth of Virginia. Eager if uncoordinated action could not wait — Virginia's and Madison County's eagerness to clinch the summer White House, eagerness of the now thoroughly alerted U. S. Marines to tackle a training task that would be genuinely special.

It is obvious in retrospect that there were several different balls in play, but it is equally obvious that the Marines under Maj. Long (now Maj. Gen. Earl C. Long, USMC, Retired) moved swiftly to bring the situation under control. When the blitz appeared to be over the hump in June 1929, Long made this revealing comment: "With one exception this was the most difficult task in my career as an engineer, covering about 25 years. Worst was in Nicaragua where I had to use pack animals to transport materials across high mountains. It would have been easier to have moved an army of 10,000 men across the Blue Ridge than to have built this camp. I have been amazed to find so wild an area existing here so close to the eastern cities."

The problem was not the eager confusion. Actually (again in retrospect) that helped. The primary problem was one of logistics. Madison County's 327 square miles held fewer than ten thousand people, almost entirely engaged in agriculture. Roads were few and slow even in the developed areas, and the western third of the county was virtually roadless and populated only by scattered mountain families. The land rose in complex folds from the Piedmont Plateau at approximately 700 feet elevation to the crest of the Blue Ridge where passes generally exceeded 3,000 feet and peaks rose above 4,000.

From a distance the ridges and hollows, even the peaks, appeared smoothly rounded, but this was a trick of camouflage performed by vegetation. Under the canopy of leaves the ancient rocks resisted efforts to build roads and run power and phone lines as, for hundreds of millions of years, they had resisted nature's weathering. Slopes that appeared to be ramps revealed themselves as stairways of cliffs. In many places soil was but a carpet over bedrock, elsewhere it was filled with boulders that might, after efforts to gouge them out, prove larger than pianos.

The forest had more than eighty different species of trees, at least that many more shrubs and vines, and hundreds of species of smaller plants. Each type of growth had its favorite environment, from moist soil to mere cracks in drier rocks, so that few spots were free of flora, no lines of march unencumbered by concealing curtains and tangles of wood. Penetration was more difficult in 1929 than it had been in 1700, for cutting of the larger trees had opened the way for denser growth, thorny berry canes, the natural barbwire of smilax, small trees so close-ranked as to constitute a barricade.

Here and there larger trees survived, such as on the specific site chosen by Hoover. Beneath those hemlocks, tulips and maples were a few shady openings where tents might be pitched or cabins constructed, but the upstream selection had lengthened the needed lines of access. The remoteness and ruggedness of upper Rapidan terrain was reflected on a 20-foot contour map produced by the U. S. Geological Survey almost before Hoover could say, "That's where I want my camp." Richey and Carson then discussed rerouting of the new road so it would ultimately serve national park purposes, not Camp Hoover alone. Richey arranged to furnish ten-ton tractors, and Carson claimed to have all road builders "stepping on the gas."

Spring came in as a friend, encouraging all kinds of work and the moving in of Marines, then turned hostile and made mud pies of newly graded earth, grinding torrents of streams. When weather quieted and warmed, there were snakes. According to Madison legend, Long fought copperheads and rattlesnakes with truckloads of hogs, his men herding these snake-eaters along access routes and into the camp area itself. Lou K. Witcofski (Captain, MSC U. S. Navy, Retired), a hospital corpsman then, vividly remembers rattlesnakes. "Marines kept one in a cage," he said. "We gave it ether and pulled its fangs. When blasting started for Skyline Drive on the mountain crest, rattlesnakes came down in droves. But we never had a snakebite case."

On May 6 the Madison County *Eagle*, after a period of relative somnolence, was jolted by a news dispatch originating in the nation's capital. As a result of "working day and night" the direct phone line had reached the campsite, and at 6 p.m. that Sunday a call had been put through to Washington. The re-alerted paper probed the all-out campaign during the next four days and prepared a multi-column story for its May 10 issue, revealing that:

A second detachment of 50 Marines was arriving to supplement a first detachment which, unpublicized, was already working at the campsite.

Lumber and equipment were already stored at Wolftown and as far up the river as Graves Mill, a nearer approach to the campsite proving possible there at that stage than on the Criglersville front.

Wooden buildings (not just the dining room-kitchen) would start rising on the Hoover site very soon.

Ennis Gilbert, foreman, had three camps of 40 men each on the Criglersville-Quaker Run route. Despite the streams having been out of their banks most of the time since early April, completion of the lengthened route (now estimated at 10 miles) was expected by June 1... A Criglersville resident reported the road project as a "sight to see." A quick survey had located a route over Chapman Mountain, aiming to limit elevation change to only seven feet in one hundred. Equipment had converged from far and near, and bosses had gone into the countryside recruiting labor. Right of way was cleared and blasted, and soon the drive was augmented by military crawler-tractors pulling heavy graders, smoothing over and between the blast holes. Timber bridges were being constructed with amazing speed, one a hundred feet long. A thousand feet of culvert was being laid for drainage. Work was proceeding at dozens of locations simultaneously.

Maj. Long and Sheriff Hall had selected an airport location on the D. S. Berry place near Syria. They were planning buildings there and estimating that urgent mail could soon leave Washington, land at the Berry Field, and be relayed to Camp Hoover to arrive within an hour and a half of transmittal.

The *Eagle* eye did not penetrate the Richey-Carson-Long lines of communication, which would have forecast things to come and sometimes explained them, but during the next three months the Madison weekly seldom failed to carry exultant reports of phenomenal advances. Some of the articles, filled with local pride, occupied four full columns on the front page and continued to the back or inside, though the total paper was only eight pages.

May 17 — Quaker Run road progressing swiftly, more bridges being built despite high water... Phone poles are 35 feet tall, crossbars designed for ten wires but only four strung now, their copper shining in the sun up to three miles away (according to T. B. Clore, Criglersville)... Work under way on Hoover Cabin, lumber moving directly upriver on primitive route negotiable only by military-type trucks. Ten 600-gallon tanks, to store pure mountain spring water for summer White House, already at the site... Marines building roads inside upper Rapidan preserve (but not involved on Criglersville access route)...

May 24 — The President slept the night of May 18 in one of five brown Army tents with wooden floors in place (situated above confluence of prongs out of the way of construction now proceeding at fast rate on "White House" itself)...

Hoover did not fish but tramped the country, accompanied by Richey, Boone, Ray Lyman Wilbur (Secretary of the Interior), and a magazine writer named Lowry...

One truck carrying food and tents got lost en route, arriving four hours late, so Hoover and guests took potluck with Marine garrison...

Grounds "have been cleaned up and leveled in places and the natural floral display made orderly and more pleasing.

Walkways have been bordered with the rocks which lay helter-skelter on the preserve. Other rocks have been erected in conical piles from which native flowers send forth their fragrance..." Flagstaff up — for U. S. flag and, when President in camp, his special flag... A massive open-air fireplace and chimney already erected...

Associated Press, Washington, reported Monday: "President Hoover today has a black eye — from weekend in Virginia. While walking along the bank of Rapidan River, Mr. Hoover stumbled over a rock and the eye came into forcible contact with a low-hanging tree limb. It was treated at once by Lt. Commander Boone but in spite of this the discoloration developed rapidly."

AP also reported Hoover and party returned from Madison County to the capital via Shenandoah Valley on Sunday morning, stopping without advance notice to attend services at the Baptist Church in Earlysville. There was only Sunday school that day, no "preaching." The children sang Hoover's favorite hymns.

This building called "Five Tents" was originally just that, five tents pitched on a wooden floor. (Capt. Lou K. Witcofski)

May 31 — Estimated $30,000 paid for Madison labor already in connection with Hoover Camp... Many visitors converging on Madison and the Rapidan from surrounding areas, the preserve being closed only when the Hoovers are there or soon expected...

Quaker Run road into the Rapidan "negotiable" now... Power line to reach camp June 1... Two famous cooks of the Marines, Sgt. C. E. White and Cpl. T. G. Monroe, selected to prepare meals for President and guests temporarily. They prepared last Saturday trout caught to order by Madison County fisherman Phil Kite, the President not having time to catch them himself...

"That river was called Rapid Anne — but no reflection on England's queen. It's the river that's fast and turbulent, hence not just Anne but Rapid Anne — later shortened to Rapidan."

June 14 — With the President and Mrs. Hoover this past Saturday, Secretary of Agriculture Arthur M. Hyde, Dr. Vernon S. Kellogg, and others — total 16 including Secret Service, White House attaches and servants. Fourteen more, including chauffeurs and various newspapermen, put up at Hunton Inn...

June 21 — Maj. Long estimates the important work planned for this year will be completed in July... Mark Sullivan a guest. Hyde again.

June 30 — Mrs. Hoover broadcast from camp this past Saturday to boys and girls all over the United States, even to Hawaii, on a 4-H Club program...

July 12 — Mrs. Hoover rode horseback to the top of the Blue Ridge with party including Dr. Kellogg, who is permanent secretary of the National Research Council, also Mark Sullivan and William Hard, news writers...

Mr. Hoover did not fish. The trout season expired July 1, and he feels it applies to him as well as to the humblest citizen... Mrs. Hoover drove one of the cars back to Washington herself, no chauffeur...

The president is expected tomorrow with members of the new Federal Farm Board. Large rooms are now available in buildings, with the smell of freshly sawed pine, should weather or insects make outdoor conferences uncomfortable...

July 26 — Hoover road (from Criglersville up Quaker Run, over Chapman Mountain ridge and upriver to Camp

(3 different views of The President's cabin) The President's cabin was "shoehorned" in among trees, some of which were left growing through porches. (NPS)

Hoover) now virtually completed. Only about 12 men left working. Cost of the longer road about $25,000, nearly double original estimate...

Pool construction and horseshoe pitching occupied last weekend's party. Hoover served as architect and chief engineer in constructing the dam to form the pool...Hoover didn't pitch horseshoes but watched.. Secretary of State Henry L. Stimson and Mrs. Stimson were there, also former Gov. Huntley Spaulding of New Hampshire.

August 2 — White House cars drove all the way to the recently completed Hoover cabin for the first time... In party were Secretary of War James Good and several assistant secretaries including Patrick J. Hurley. Purpose of conference: to reduce costs of Army, save money, cut taxes. A detailed study and discussion. Hoover's first chance for real attack on this problem — and most intensive use of the camp for a governmental conference thus far...

August 9 — Hoover himself prepared ham and eggs for supper Saturday. Among those present: Postmaster General Walter F. Brown, Attorney General William D. Mitchell, F. T. Hines (head of Veterans Bureau), Senator Reed Smoot, and both of the Hoover sons...

About 400 men on the preserve now, also many horses and mules and much modern machinery...Charles A. Lindbergh and wife expected this coming weekend...

Much the same story of Camp Hoover's swift growth and early operation was told in other papers, though without the intimate detail of the voluminous *Eagle* articles and minus the local pride. Some important factors were overlooked, or inadequately emphasized, the press tending to show Hoover as being showered by benefits from all sides. As President, carrying heavy burdens for the people, he may be considered to have deserved whatever legal benefits came his way, but seeing the camp situation more completely shows the man as far more interesting.

Congress had appropriated $48,000 to provide a summer White House in the mountains. Hoover refused to spend the money.

Virginia, through its conservation and development commission headed by Carson, offered to build a Presidential lodge costing about $100,000. Hoover declined the offer. Finally realizing the President was not to be persuaded, Carson included these words in a letter to him of August 2, 1929: "Our only regret has been that you have not felt at liberty to accept the title deeds to the property, together with a suitable building properly equipped and ready for your use, as an evidence of the hospitality and good will with which the people of Virginia welcome your occasional visits."

Though the rapid road construction served Hoover's needs, he so guided it through Richey that it also served long-range county and state interests. Madison County today credits Hoover with providing key impetus for its modern highway network.

The War Department proposed to send U. S. Army Engineer troops to widen and gravel the new access road, but Hoover agreed only after receiving a letter from the Secretary of War (dated August 14) explaining that the troops regularly engaged in road work as training and "no expense incurred would be other than a proper charge against the training of troops."

Hoover personally bought (from the Wayland estate at $5 an acre, the prevailing price then) the land on which the camp was situated, and he personally paid approximately $15,000 for building materials and supplies. Many years afterward, to clarify for all time a question which kept coming up, General Long wrote to the superintendent of Shenandoah National Park: "Mr. Hoover paid for all materials and supplies, including food stuffs used in the camp. Of course he didn't pay transportation or construction costs. This was provided by the Marines, who constructed the President's Camp, the Cabinet Camp, and their own camp — and at the same time carried out considerable military training..."

Long's second-most-difficult task and the eager helpfulness from others which accompanied it are thus revealed as costing no one, except Hoover himself, anything which would not otherwise have been spent, perhaps for purposes less useful. Even the extensions of power and phone lines by the utility corporations were repaid many times over through charges resulting from Presidential use. Long, a central figure during camp establishment, was directly responsible for buildings as well as for water supply and sewage disposal and for intra-camp roadways and trails.

In an informational letter of May 1, 1931, he pointed out that "extremely simple designs" were followed for all buildings, "which in the President's camp proper total ten and afford accommodations for 24 guests." There were two water systems, one for drinking and culinary water originating in a covered spring and never chlorinated, the other drawing from an open stream for uses such as fire protection, baths and showers, and always chlorinated.

Many years later in his *Memoirs*, Hoover referred to the buildings as "log cabins," but they were actually made of pine boards, adequate but not showy heavy framing covered by what has been called "German siding." There were no ceilings and the roofs were thin, meant to exclude precipitation but not to hold heat. The structures were described as comfortable for spring, summer and fall use but without architectural distinction — except the massive field-stone chimneys. Commenting on the fact that the fireplaces never smoked, one experienced builder explained "this was not so much because they were well built, which they were, but because they were so big, hence sucked so hard, the buildings being more or less open to air, never intended to be kept warm in cold weather."

The Hoovers had so quickly become fond of the Rapidan that they telescoped the tent-village idea with their dream of a more permanent camp, all within a few weeks in 1929. First structure was Five Tents (120 by 30 feet, its canvas later replaced by wood), followed by the President's "Brown House," soon called simply The President. This lodge had a living room 60 by 20 feet, two bedrooms, two baths, a screened sleeping porch, a large sitting porch with a big tree left growing through its floor. Marines boasted that the larger of two fireplaces required 51 tons of rock.

Then came the Mess Hall (with a "galley" and outdoor grill at back) and quarters up the slope for the Navy men (a chief steward and a dozen Filipino cooks and attendants) who operated the Presidential mess serving the entire camp. Next came Town Hall, for indoor conferences and recreation, and the small Office (or "duty shack"), center for the Secret Service and for Marines aiding in camp protection and emergency maintenance. Construction continued at a less frenzied pace, adding guest cabins until the basic complex of rustic structures, spaced widely among the trees, was completed. (See pictorial map for complete lay-out.)

The number of men under Long's command approached 500 in mid-1929, partly needed for the speedy construction,

The Town Hall was a center for conferences and recreation. (NPS)

partly for Presidential protection, and partly for military training on the mountains. The Marines established their own camp a mile east of Camp Hoover itself. This Marine Camp was almost entirely tents for several years, the only buildings being the mess hall, the commander's office, and the sick bay. Typical contingent during periods of Presidential presence was 150-250 Marines (plus one Navy hospital corpsman "to take care of the injured and sick, lame and lazy"). In winter there were only about a dozen Marines (and the hospital corpsman).

Many of the Marines were selected for their skill in carpentry, plumbing, and related work. Part of the Camp Hoover furniture was "homemade" on the spot by Marines, and Long proudly claimed this furniture "had one quality I will vouch for, sturdiness." Hoover hired men to blaze and build hiking trails and bridle paths to peaks, waterfalls, and other scenic places, but the Marines did work of this kind too, along with odd jobs of wide variety.

Long remained in command throughout the Hoover administration. Like the Hoovers, he had a California background and, as others of the inner circle commented with a touch of jealousy, "spoke the lingo." He and his wife occupied

In The President's cabin—Mrs. Edgar Ricard ("Abbe"), Phillipi Butler (Mrs. Fred Butler, one of Mrs. Hoover's secretaries), Mrs. Hoover, Dare McMullin, a Filipino houseboy, and, to the right of the fireplace, Major Earl C. Long of the U. S. Marine Corps. (Adm. Joel T. Boone)

one of the President's cabins and were with the Hoovers for meals and frequently for recreation. Long developed a lasting dedication to the Chief. It is told of him that, in future projects including construction of military posts, he always protected natural conditions to the maximum possible extent. Just as he had, upon Hoover instructions, built the porch of the President's cabin around the trunk of a living tree, he frequently modified military plans to avoid cutting trees.

Paul C. Abernethy (a retired Chief Warrant Officer now living in Piedmont Virginia), who was in charge of maintenance at Camp Hoover for several years, also became conservation-minded. He remembers building a fountain under Mrs. Hoover's direction. It was round with steps rising toward a narrow apex where the water would gush out, each step a circular goldfish bowl. Waterproof concrete was used as mortar, but the natural-stone appearance had to dominate. Water had to be piped from an open stream, and Mrs. Hoover insisted on the very minimum of disturbance of natural stream structure and on careful replacement of both vegetation and rocks

The Slums where many of the guests stayed. (NPS)

over the pipeline. Only dead wood, mostly blight-killed chestnut, could be used for cooking and heating in the Hoover years — no living trees, no coal or oil.

Outdoor lights were placed high in trees, hidden by foliage so as to reduce the appearance of artificiality (perhaps also to entice insects away from the walkways). This led to problems. Since light was essential in protection of the Hoovers and their eminent guests, Abernethy once had to climb a very high ladder in a thunderstorm to fix a light that had failed. When he came down, his waiting captain said, "You know, I wouldn't have gone up there for five thousand dollars!"

"So you sent me!"

"Duty," the captain philosophized. "We all have duties. That happened to be one of mine."

Abernethy also recalls helping transport trout into the high country. "We always let the mountain water into the containers gradually," he said, "giving the fish time to adjust to the cold."

Marines were a continuing, if slightly detached, part of the Hoover community. They adopted the long-standing designation of Hoover as the Chief, or simply as Chief, and went along with secretaries and friends in referring to Mrs. Hoover as Lady or The Lady . Some who, one way or another, became personally known to the Chief or the Lady, heard from them at intervals for years after their time at camp.

Marines' guard tents in a blizzard. (Capt. Lou K. Witcofski)

A constant duty of the Marines was protection. A company of 50 under a Lt. Bell was the President's official guard. It had been transferred from the yacht Mayflower as soon as Hoover began using the camp, and it was always ready on the Rapidan when the Chief was there. Long's instructions to the men under him were printed in a 120-page booklet, *Detachment Regulations and Orders for the Guard,* which he later explained he had "compiled to insure security and service for the camp, and cooperation with the Secret Service." Excerpts help illuminate camp conditions:

> This mission ... is to furnish adequate protection for the Commander in Chief, and to construct, maintain, and guard the necessary camps comprising Camp Rapidan...
>
> Pistols in use by the guard will be signed for by each sergeant of the guard and kept locked in the box provided for that purpose... When the President is in, the quartermaster will report all available transporation to the officer of the day, who will then be responsible for the transportation needed until the President leaves...
>
> Drivers will sound horn at all blind curves on the road

Meals were prepared in the "galley" (at rear, left) and served in the Mess Hall. (NPS)

between Criglersville and the camp... Coasting in or out of gear is prohibited...

While the President's party is in camp, drivers of motor vehicles, especially class D drivers, will proceed on the main road between the Marine Camp, Camp 3, and the President's Camp at a speed much more reduced than ordinarily... Drivers nearing the vicinity of the "White House," or upon entering the President's Camp will not blow their horns unnecessarily. Drivers taking mail to the President's Camp will proceed at their usual rate of speed... When driving down Chapman Mountain toward Camp Rapidan, all drivers will shift in a low gear and will remain in this gear until within 100 yards of the sentry box at the Graves Mill Road...

Horse orderlies for White House parties will be in the prescribed uniform and will present a neat and military appearance. Orderlies will use the back road when reporting or returning to the corral with animals... When the President is in camp all available horses will be held saddled at the corral at 9:30 a.m. and 2 p.m. daily... Horse orderlies accompanying the President's guests will proceed to the head of the column when approaching a gate to be opened, but will do so at a moderate rate of speed...

No visitors will be admitted to the President's Camp except Marines and Navy personnel on duty, without a pass signed by: (a) Mr. Lawrence Richey, (b) the commanding officer...

The telephone lineman inspecting the mountain telephone line prior to the arrival of the President will also inspect the fish rack, and will clear same if necessary...

No trees in the President's Camp or the guard camp areas (including first and second platoon areas, corral area, and motor transport area) will be cut, damaged, or limbs removed, except by the authority of the commanding officer...

At 8 a.m. daily when the President is in and at least two hours before his arrival on days when he is expected, the switchboard operator on watch will test all camp telephones by ringing each one, receiving a ring on each one, and talking over each one... The radio repair man will check all radio sets in the President's Camp on Thursday for their proper functioning, making any minor repairs immediately...

Fishing in the Rapidan is prohibited without special permission from the commanding officer...

Farm houses and orchards are out of bounds unless permission is granted by the owner to enter...

Members of this command will not swim or bathe in rivers or streams in the vicinity of Camp Rapidan without permission of the commanding officer...

The Marine Camp later acquired amenities, such as this recreation hall. (Capt. Lou K. Witcofski)

Unless a member of the Secret Service is present, the duty officer will keep himself advised of Mrs. Hoover's whereabouts, and will send an orderly to follow her at about 50 yards when she goes for a walk outside the camp. When Mrs. Hoover is in camp the duty officer will not leave the President's Camp to go to meals unless a Secret Service man will be present during his absence...

A road patrol consisting of 1 officer, 1 pickup driver, 1 telephone lineman, a corporal, and 3 sentries will close the road 2 hours and 15 minutes after the President leaves Washington for camp. The same patrol will close the road 15 minutes before the President leaves Camp Rapidan for Washington...

Orders were listed for eleven different sentry posts in and around camp. Seven special sentries were posted along the access road when the President was arriving or leaving. Detailed instructions were given for flag signaling in case telephones went out of order. Officers were instructed to "warn your sentries to be prepared to carry out any unexpected orders, *even to the extent of stopping the President's car.*"

Elaborate precautions were taken against unauthorized persons and against fire. Marines assisted Virginia authorities in construction of a fire tower on top of Fork Mountain (3852 feet above sea level). The tower gave a full view of the camp area, and it was manned by Marines whenever dryness indicated possibility of forest fires. Airplanes were used for supplementary fire-watching, especially when haze thickened on Fork Mountain. People from Camp Hoover climbed to use the tower for scenic viewing, and some said they could see the Washington Monument through binoculars on the clearest days. An elderly mountain woman told camp personnel that Fork Mountain had been used during the War Between the States for sending heliograph signals direct to Washington.

An airplane brought urgent mail from Washington when the President was in camp and was sometimes used also for return mail and for guests (never the Hoovers) who needed to return to the capital quickly. A cleared area at Broyles Gap about a mile above the Marine Camp soon made possible even faster mail service by receiving dropped bags. A pick-up squad in the mail-plane Ford went to this field before the plane's arrival and displayed wind panels to help guide drops. They could also signal the pilot in some detail — the letters EI laid out on the field, for example, meant "land at Syria for mail

Urgent mail was dropped from the air. (Capt. Lou K. Witcofski)

or passenger."

The Hoover period on the Rapidan was without spectacular threats or emergencies. Several Marine vehicles struck cows, and one truck carrying Marines tipped over, but these accidents occurred on the populated Piedmont, not in the mountains. The President's health was so persistently good that frustrated newsmen had to content themselves, on this score, with such trivial stories as that about a black eye. Herbert Hoover, Jr. however, developed tuberculosis and spent many weeks in Five Tents, leaving for care and treatment elsewhere only when winter closed the camp.

Marines experienced some mild hostility. Jim Colvin of Milam Gap, one of the mountain "farmers" who let their hogs run wild to fatten on acorns and other natural food including snakes, appeared near camp one day in an angry mood. "I hear you soldiers 're shootin' hogs!" he accused a sentry. "You better not a shot mine!"

The Marine countered, "You can't carry a gun here, fella!"

"No? Allus have!" But Colvin soon decided against taking on the Marines and left to look elsewhere for his hogs, ultimately finding them nearer home.

It was true that the Marines shot "wild hogs," about fifty over a period of several years, as they were a destructive nuisance and somewhat dangerous to man. Abernethy told of using a 30-30 rifle in this duty, of strict orders the hogs could not be used, and of the crew with picks and shovels assigned to follow the "hunter" and bury the carcasses. This operation must have been kept secret from the Hoovers. Whether all hogs shot were from truckloads previously released by Long to reduce the snake population (if that legend was actually based on truth), or whether mountaineers' hogs were sometimes shot, will never be definitely known.

The air postman, returning to Washington after a mail drop, once noticed a burning house on the Piedmont. He gave an alarm by circling until the roar of the plane drew attention. One neighbor said the plane imitated "a mother bird in distress over its nest being robbed — alarmed for the safety of its fledglings." Soon the roads leading to the burning house were filled with speeding aid.

Mrs. Hoover, while driving near Culpeper, also once spotted a fire. She and her party stopped and helped carry valuables from the house. She drove the family into town and bought clothes for them. They did not know who she was, and she did not tell.

Upon the initiative of Secretaries Wilbur and Hyde and Attorney General Mitchell, a Cabinet Camp was constructed by the Marines about two miles downstream from the President's camp, and there was a flurry of unpleasantness in 1931 over that site. Associated Press reported on June 8 that "the Cabinet Camp ... intended for use of cabinet members coming down to confer with the executive, was claimed today by the Ward-Rue Lumber Company." The firm's representatives had appeared before state commissioners meeting at Madison for condemnation of land to be included in Shenandoah National Park. They claimed timber holdings valued in excess of $1 million and said the Cabinet Camp was on their land without a lease ever signed.

Papers next day carried a White House statement denying "that private land was seized for the erection of a camp for cabinet members," declaring that "the land had been obtained by oral permission from the owners." The site was improved with six buildings, water pipes and roadway — which, according to the White House estimate, cost $5,000, but which Ward-Rue valued at $20,000.

Drew Pearson probed and concluded: (1) The dispute did not touch the President's camp which was on 164 acres owned by Hoover personally and surrounded by 2,000 acres leased by Hoover personally. (2) It did not touch the Marine Camp for which Maj. Long had a definite lease (though just possibly the horse corral extended 15 feet over the line). (3) It was a toss-up whether the cabinet members had been slip-shod in making their land contract, or whether the landowners were trying to capitalize on the President's presence near them to extract too large a share of the Shenandoah National Park fund. And (4) Marines had halted Ward-Rue people and by show of force prevented them from entering this portion of their own land. (A fact missed by Drew Pearson, and possibly the basic explanation, was that the state conservation com-mission had arranged for "additional campsites without charge on the lands of Ward-Rue Lumber Company" — quoting a letter of May 18, 1929, from Carson to Long with copy to Richey.)

The run-in with the Marines was probably the initiating cause of the flurry. But the owners might have been more tolerant, even have laughed off the whole matter, if they had known that the same thing had happened in August 1929 to — of all people! — Carson. A newly arrived Marine interpret-ed his instructions literally and refused persuasion. (Next time Carson had a pass signed by Richey.)

The Ward-Rue representatives soon explained they had mentioned the Cabinet Camp only to make known it was on their land, not to embarrass cabinet members or anyone else. This sounded like an apology. But in July the *Eagle* reported a sign prohibiting trucks from using the "Hoover Mountain Road" without permission from the state conservation com-mission. The paper protested that the "posted" road was pub-lic, having been built by state and county funds, and that the sign was intended to forestall timber-cutting by Ward-Rue on Rapidan lands.

No trucks came, however, and there was no obvious tim-ber cutting. The flurry subsided without clear settlement. Cabinet members continued to occupy the camp through the Hoover administration, and Ward-Rue resumed the preroga-tives of ownership when the cottages were no longer in use. The Ward-Rue lands never were acquired for the national park as the purchase fund ran low and minimum park acreage was reduced by Congress. In 1953 the Cabinet cabins were bought by a Washington co-op named Rapidan Camps, Inc.

"Our objective," explained the leader of the group, "is to develop a cool, attractive and economical vacation retreat. Other people with similar interests are welcome to join our project."

Cabinet members, incidentally, had avoided fishing in competition with Hoover along the Rapidan. Secretaries Wilbur and Hyde obtained control of fishing rights to Hazel River (northward in the proposed park) and arranged to have that stream stocked with seven-inch trout.

Intoxicating liquor was firmly frowned upon by Mr. and Mrs. Hoover (only in part because prohibition was then the law of the land), and never during the Hoover period was there evidence of liquor or drunkeness in the President's camp. A supposedly well informed Marine declared, however, that in the surrounding mountain country "there was moonshine in every stump-hole if you knew how to look for it." Others mentioned "excellent applejack" made by a mountain man "who lived not so very far down the river."

The Marines' acquaintance with the mountain folk became extensive and in many cases lasting. Some Marines married their mountain girl-friends and, according to best available information, lived quite happily ever after.

III

Nature and the Neighbors

Mrs. Hoover's influence at camp was constant, and, partly because she was not directly weighted down by the nation's worries as was her husband, she ranged more widely and became more familiar with the natural features and the people.

Mrs. Hoover explored extensively on horseback.
(Herbert Hoover Presidential Library)

Despite an amount of "help" that would have overwhelmed a lesser character, she continued to come through strongly as wife and hostess. The Navy, through the Filipinos transferred from the former Presidential yacht Mayflower, operated the kitchen and dining room. Cooking utensils and serving dishes from the yacht formed the basis of the camp's culinary equipment. But the meals were Hoover meals.

A typical camp breakfast was bacon and eggs, hot cakes and coffee. Luncheon was often a snack eaten during a brief rest from fishing, hiking, riding, or working. Dinner was frequently broiled steaks or chops, or chicken, or Rapidan fish, roasted potatoes and coffee. Hoover coffee was made with one tablespoonful for each cup, and one more added for good measure, tied in a cloth and lowered into the boiling water.

Women guests were likely to have brought dinner dresses, but opportunities to wear them were few. Mrs. Hoover might say shortly before dinner, "I'm going to put on something warmer now, so we can walk out and see the moon and listen to the stream, and perhaps hear the tree frogs singing." The men often wore white flannels, weather permitting. Hoover did not wear formal clothes at camp but always appeared neat.

Primarily because Mrs. Hoover liked to ride, horses were kept ready. While Mr. Hoover fished alone, Mrs. Hoover liked company on her excursions, so guests more often found recreation with the Lady than with the Chief. Sometimes she had

Mrs. Hoover was President of the Girl Scouts of America and entertained both leaders and girls in the Blue Ridge. (Underwood & Underwood, Library of Congress)

Girl Scouts as guests. Her wide range from camp is illustrated by a Girl Scout excursion she planned into Shenandoah Valley, taking care to plot a route on which horses would not have to tread hard-surface roads.

There were forms of recreation which neither of the Hoovers joined. Dr. Boone was a rider, mountain climber, and dam builder. He was also a fisherman, though not in the President's and Richey's class. Boone and Richey initiated games of horseshoes, or tackled jigsaw puzzles, drawing guests in with them. There was a ping-pong table in Town Hall. Both President and Mrs. Hoover were voluminous readers of a wide variety of books, as well as newspapers and magazines, and the camp soon became a library with reading material circulating from cabin to cabin.

Mr. Hoover was inclined toward combinations of recreation and work. Fishing was an example (creative thinking an accompaniment to the casting, the waiting, the movement of the water). His reading was in the same category unless he was especially tired. Boulder-gathering and dam-building to create pools was one of these double-pronged schemes into which he often drew guests, Cabinet members, congressmen, diplomats, bankers, men representing the whole spectrum of American life with whom communication was generally stimulated through informality.

Admiral Boone, reminiscing about the camp, recently said, "President and Mrs. Hoover complemented each other — a perfect team. I never heard a voice raised between them,

The Hoovers' beds were made by the Marines. (Adm. Joel T. Boone)

A "corner" in Town Hall, suitable for reading, games, or light conversation.
(Adm. Joel T. Boone)

though each had highly intelligent and individualistic mental processes. She called him 'Daddy' and he called her 'Lou.' They walked together in-and out-of-doors...

"The President never said a word about criticism of himself, which rose to a high pitch during his administration. But Mrs. Hoover resented it and felt it deeply. Women understand how she felt — he was her man...

"Both were remarkably generous — but often independently. I never heard of anyone more generous than President Hoover — to Blue Ridge people in need, for example. But he never talked of such matters, nor did she — it would have been a breach of etiquette. Mrs. Hoover never told what she did with her money, but after her death it was learned she had been helping many girls through college..."

Philippi H. Butler, then a secretary, remembers the "Lady" also helped boys and whole families: "All appeals sent to her during the Depression were carefully handled in an effort to provide help through friends or appropriate organizations. She often contributed money anonymously after receiving a report that the appeal was perfectly genuine and special help was deserved."

44

Mrs. Hoover hung maps of the camp and its vicinity, including trails, in all the cabins, along with information sheets which read:

Cabins have no bells. If you want anything you will have to tell a Filipino boy beforehand, or ask the orderly at the "Office" to send for one for you.

Cabins have side shutters that let down from outside, if you want more air.

Cabins have a two-bath heater (if the first bath isn't too full!). The third bath must be waited for for about 20 minutes.

"The Owl," a guest cabin. (NPS)

Cabins have drinking (spring) water in the taps.

The Town Hall in the center of the camp is the place of general meeting for anything from Executive Committee Meeting to ping-pong and knitting.

First Aid — There is a "Chief Pharmacist's Mate" at the Marine Camp who can attend to brusies, poison oak (which we don't have) and such. He also can supply ordinary drugs. When in doubt about *anything whatever* ask Major Long (or call a conference of your nearest neighbors).

Meals are served in the Mess Hall — usually! For safety follow your nose's guidance or the movement of the population.

Meals are served fifteen minutes after the warning bell, to those who arrive. Others eat when they are ready!

For directions, look at the camp map in your cabin and consult your compass!

When cold at night, after all blankets and eiders are exhausted, put on your camel's hair dressing gown, wrap your head in a sweater, and throw your fur coat over everything!

Complete absence of poison oak (or ivy) which the information sheet claimed represented a remarkable victory. Within the realm of the natural, Mrs. Hoover was subtly transforming the floral pattern, encouraging species congenial to man, discouraging the uncongenial. She gave high priority to learning the camp environment in all its facets, first asking questions of those who should know, then pushing personal investigations. The Virginia education department furnished books and other information about birds, trees, mammals, fish, snakes, and the human history in which the Rapidan had been involved, and Mrs. Hoover made the materials obviously available at camp.

Her constant botanizing proved contagious. One friend remembers bringing her specimens for identification and, on two occasions, having them sent on to the greenhouse man at the White House because even Mrs. Hoover did not know them. "She would have loved this book," the friend added, speaking of *Wildflowers in Color*, recently published to help identify prominent species from Shenandoah to Great Smokies parks. "She would have placed copies in all the cottages. She would have had it in Girl Scout Little House in Washington."

Mrs. Hoover's botanizing persisted even when she was driving a car, and she sometimes startled passengers by swerving or braking to get a better look at a plant beside the road. She was responsible for gay flower boxes that brightened the cabins, and around the grounds she made natural-looking flower pots of fallen logs and rocks. A copy of her seven-page directions, "Flowers and Shrubs for the President's Camp," has come down to us. It began:

> The President requested that a very great many kinds of plants, flowers, etc. be prepared to be taken up to camp and set out whenever the different seasons permit. (The President said that a couple, or as many as necessary, gardeners could come up from the White House and put the plants in. Major Long says that the Marine detail, after the plants have been set out, can be taught by the gardener how to weed and cultivate them from day to day. At occasional intervals — perhaps once a

fortnight — a gardener could go up from here and see how things are going, give further directions to the Marines if necessary...)

The plants taken up want to be either the identical species which grow in that neighborhood (within a radius of 20 to 25 miles) or of perhaps hardy species that might be better to cultivate but very similar to the native ones. (For instance, there is a native forget-me-not and a little native plant that is not a lily-of-the-valley but looks remarkably like one. But the cultivated species of these two can well be put in at camp.) All the plants should be such as not to seem out of place among that woodsy setting.

The President is very fond of color in gardens so where possible *and appropriate to the species*, arrange the flowering shrubs and flowers so as to give mass effects of color.

President and Mrs. Hoover often walked together, sometimes hand-in-hand. (Library of Congress)

The immediate surroundings of the camp have many trees and bushes, which means a great deal of shade; yet there are open spaces where the sun comes through, so that these patches can be picked out for sun-loving things. But there must be a great many things for blooming in the shady places. NOTE: There should be no formal beds of plants or flowers but, while having a certain compactness so as to give masses of color, should ramble off into the surroundings. They should not be carefully trimmed, nor should the beds be outlined in any way.

Some flowers should be planted right along the creek's edge, others overhanging the water...

Also Mrs. Hoover does want to have planted, in addition to all the foregoing, a little distance from the camp either in open places or shade as the flowering plants demand, considerable numbers of plants (probably the same type as those about camp)*whose flowers can be used for cutting.* She does not like to cut the plants that are inside around the camp, yet she wants flowers for bowls in the cabins. So by putting little semi-beds in nearby localities, they can raise the flowers for table use in the various cottages, and yet have them "wild-like" flowers, not the rose and carnation type from the White House.

NOTE: While there are plenty of shrubs and a profusion of ferns in the neighborhood that can be transplanted into the camp's grounds, the President and Mrs. Hoover are *very* insistent that no ferns or other plants be taken from points in the vicinity that would be frequented by them or their guests (i.e., they should not be taken from along a creek, trail or open meadow, but from little hidden-away places...)

Mrs. Hoover does not wish an extravagant or exorbitant outlay made for any one particular species, unless consulted before the purchase is made. (For instance, if this is the wrong time of the year to get forget-me-not seed and to do so would mean spending several dollars more per pound, let her know of the difference in total cost before buying the seed.)

There were lists of flowers and shrubs most desired — *"get all* of these unless *very* expensive" — or, wanted *"if* easily obtained and easily grown" — or, already profuse in the neighborhood and to be encouraged in camp — or, to be found within a few miles and transplanted *"if* the camp soil is found to be suitable as might be judged by the kind of trees present in camp, including nuts (hickory, walnut, etc.), hemlock

"Hemlock Run," a small stream with waterfalls, was created by a diversion dam on Laurel Prong. (Adm. Joel T. Boone)

(many), pine (few), yew (few), gums, tulips, maples (few), chestnuts (blighted), oaks."

Mrs. Hoover noted that mountain laurel was present in "wonderful profusion" but called attention to the absence in the camp itself of honeysuckle, huckleberry, dogwood, rhododendrons, and Judas trees and expressed the hope these missing species might be brought in from nearby. Among plants she classified as most desirable were "morning glories, wild cucumber, black-eyed susans, yellow-eyed susans, butterfly weed, spireas, hardy asters, trilliums, jacks-in-the-pulpit, columbines, mimulus, goldenrod, violets, ladyslippers, Virginia creeper, common 'red' swamp lilies (almost orange color), tiger lilies, day lilies (wildish), Solomon seals (the *real* kind - much 'false' Solomon seals already present), foxgloves, gentians, iris, lupines, gourds (*all* kinds), larkspur."

Mrs. Hoover also concerned herself with furnishings. On her horseback rides she learned that Mrs. Jim Colvin, living at Milam Gap, made braided rugs. She considered such rugs especially suitable for the rustic camp, and also wished to encourage such enterprise, so at various times she bought rugs from Mrs. Colvin. (Mrs. Franklin D. Roosevelt, years later, also once bought rugs from Mrs. Colvin.)

The *Eagle* disclosed in July 1930 that Mrs. Hoover had visited the Clore furniture plant at Madison and been "impressed." She bought "two chairs minus bottoms (she and her niece were going to try bottoming them)." The paper later reported that, "as a result of widespread publicity following and amplifying our recent item about Mrs. Hoover and the Clore furniture," the Clores are getting many orders from far places. "An addition is planned for the plant."

Next spring the *Eagle* revealed that Mrs. Hoover had loaned E. A. Clore & Sons $200 on "the five-year-without-interest plan, thus uniting with Madison County citizens in financing the re-establishment of their furniture factory which was destroyed by fire last fall... Mrs. Hoover will get the first piece of furniture made in the new factory, a four-poster bed to be used in Hoover lodge in Madison County."

Happiness was warmth and flickering light from a camp fireplace.
(Adm. Joel T. Boone)

There were numerous signs the American people wanted to live the camp life vicariously with the Hoovers, though the ingrained reluctance of both the Chief and the Lady to drama-tize themselves kept the tendency down. A Pennsylvanian drove all the way to the camp and left in custody of a Filipino three rustic rocking chairs which he hoped "might be accept-able...especially as we are believers in the great cause of World

Peace and feel closely in sympathy with President Hoover's efforts at this time." A hand-hewn bowl of Philippine hardwood arrived one day by Marine truck. A tomahawk was sent, and Mrs. Hoover informed the donor it was being placed above the large fireplace.

The Virginia game commission sent two live wild turkeys. They were displayed and studied but then returned because, in Richey's words, we were "somewhat concerned about turning the turkeys loose in the woods, thinking that if this were done the natives or foxes would soon have a turkey feast." Several historic lanterns arrived for "camp use." A New York pastor sent a tablet (with a motto for fishermen) which he bought in London, and Hoover "ensconced it so all may share its benefits." A special fishing rod (with reel) was given by an association of Izaak Walton chapters — but circumstances delayed presentation beyond fishing season, so a bit of doggerel accompanied the gift, cautioning Hoover "to hang the rod on a hickory limb, and don't go near the water."

The 40-piece municipal band of Charlottesville (Virginia) sought the privilege of playing for Hoover at camp. A photographer sent a collection of prints showing scenic streams and asked if he might photograph the President on the Rapidan. Artists and writers sought permission to interpret or record scenes and activities. A master of the rare art of "wood gravure" came to make carvings for presentation to the Library of Congress. Innumerable citizens, living near and far, wanted passes to visit the camp (at times when they would not inconvenience the Hoovers), and from several states came requests for Rapidan rocks to be added to collections or rock gardens. Some requests had to be refused, but rocks were in surplus and always sent (by express).

An occasional letter fell short of complete friendliness. A New York woman wanted to know if the U. S. Marine Corps was not handicapped by lack of horses as a result of filling the Rapidan stables. The commanding general of the corps fielded that one, stating the Marines remained "adequately provided for." Actually, not all the twelve-to-fifteen horses at Rapidan belonged to the military. Hoover's Old Bill was one that did not.

Washington *Daily News*, discussing a proposed "blue law" for the District of Columbia, said the President could hardly favor it as "he has frequently gone fishing on Sunday." A flurry of letters protested this "debauchery," but the writers received a surprise. Richey was able truthfully to inform them that "the President never fishes on Sunday."

A national news service distributed a paragraph of dynamite stating that fisherman Hoover had "ordered unrestricted shooting of hoot owls and fish hawks at the Rapidan camp." The President, contrary to his usual practice, answered the first protest in the series himself. "I am at a loss to know why such trivial untruths (or large ones for that matter) are circulated... There are no hawks about the camp and the old owl and brood of little owls are a part of the treasured camp furniture." Richey sent copies to others who protested.

Mrs. Hoover (standing) and friends enjoy the naturally landscaped grounds.
(Herbert Hoover Presidential Library)

Scandal-talk spread among Izaak Walton clubs that the President, an Izaak Waltonian himself, had violated a cardinal principle by "appropriating a public fishing stream for his own exclusive use." Carson had the answer this time — that he held the Rapidan fishing rights and permitted Hoover and friends to use them, that the stream had never been public but might soon become so because of Hoover's interest in it.

Citizen reaction, in total, demonstrated pleasure in having the first family living, even if only occasionally, the outdoor life which is a long-standing part of the American ideal.

From the very beginnings of the camp, Hoover felt it was being created for future Presidents as well as for himself. In August 1929 he wrote to Carson: "I have received the title deed... This camp has come to have some public aspects, due to the many contributions in its making... I desire that the camp shall ultimately become the property of Shenandoah National Park, so that at the expiration of my term of office, they may hold it for the use of my successors for a weekend camp, or if future Presidents do not wish to avail themselves of it, it is at the disposal of the park itself. Therefore, I would be glad to either deed it now or await the transfer of the park to the Federal Government, whichever you think best."

This statement, when released, caused a paper avalanche. Historical societies praised the "great step toward preservation," and many other organizations passed and transmitted resolutions of gratitude. Individual citizens sent their thanks. Virginia newspapers editorialized on Hoover's wisdom in choosing a Virginia site and in helping Shenandoah National Park become a reality. Other papers applauded — and, further, deplored the long failure of the Government to provide its Chief Executive with a summer home near the capital. One called this failure "an example of penuriousness that is little short of a disgrace to the richest nation on earth." There were kind words for Hoover's creation of the camp "without cost to the federal treasury."

How about a game of horseshoes? (Herbert Hoover Presidential Library)

But skepticism emerged too. The Omaha *World-Herald* wrote:

> President Hoover seems to think that what is sauce for one President...must certainly be sauce for another. The United States owns a lot of pretty good fishing-holes in its national-park system, and Presidents heretofore who have liked to fish had little trouble avoiding the "No Trespassing" signs. Besides, we suppose that one could troll a line in the wake of the May-flower, if he had to, and, anyway, with a fine yacht like that to take one's self and friends to sea in, the lure of rod and reel could not be quite as strong.
>
> But Mr. Hoover ups and drydocks the yacht... And then he buys 164 acres of land up in the Rapidan with a good fishing-hole on it, right out of his own pocket, thumbing his nose at the national parks. Now he is working to improve the place "for my successors."
>
> Even though fishing seems to be the only standard of recreation for the job of President — Mr. Coolidge didn't have it, so he set out bravely to learn — it seems just possible that the "successors" of Mr. Hoover might rather do something else when they took a day off, and, even if they did decide to follow the custom and go fishing, they might take a shine to some other place...

For many days the country was discussing the recreational tastes of Presidents. The Washington *Evening Star* contrasted Coolidge's and Congress's preference for Mt. Weather with Hoover's liking for the Rapidan, then continued:

> President Harding would not have considered for a minute going to either place for a vacation. The same would have been true of Woodrow Wilson and Chief Justice Taft when he was President. Colonel Roosevelt would have enjoyed himself at either place, but he never deserted his old home, Sagamore Hill, at Oyster Bay, New York. It would be difficult, too, to picture William McKinley trying to have a good time at Mt. Weather or tramping over the mountain trails or fishing the streams around the Hoover mountain camp. The habits of Grover Cleveland suggest that he may have been tempted to go to such places occasionally, but only when trout season was open...
>
> Abraham Lincoln had little time or taste for vacation places during his occupancy of the White House. He was occupied with the conduct of the Civil War. He did, however, set

up what might be described as a summer White House in the Soldiers' Home grounds, in this city. where he went for two summers to get away from the heat...

Chester A. Arthur frequently went to the Lincoln House at Soldiers' Home for weekend parties and longer periods of rest. Most of his summers were spent at Long Branch, on the Jersey coast, as were those of President Grant. President Garfield also spent a summer at that resort. Benjamin Harrison evidently thought little of summer vacations. Invariably he went to his home in Indianapolis, Indiana, for the summer, although it is recorded that he and Mrs. Harrison spent one summer at Loon Lake in the Adirondack Mountains...

Madison County memories connect Hoover quite specifically with modern roads: "We'd been mostly in the mud, almost no surfaced highways. But additional roads had to be built to bring the camp within the 100-mile limit, and Secret Service rules didn't allow the President to travel the same route time after time, so there had to be other highways..." "Roads? Let me tell you — that Hoover deal put us in gear. They were in such a hurry for roads, they didn't take time to get right-of-way except by word-of-mouth. There's still a problem on one stretch..." "Hoover backed a road past his camp and on over the Blue Ridge. He was a real genuine road man...."

Documents give depth to these recollections. In the fall of 1929 the U. S. Bureau of Public Roads was anxious to experiment near Washington with a type of bituminous surfacing that had been markedly successful in the less-humid West. Richey suggested a road via Haywood in Madison County that would, incidentally, cut five miles off Hoover's trips to and from camp. The section was completed in record time.

That same year, in a get-together at Skyland, the resort's owner-operator, G. Freeman Pollock, and representatives of the Virginia conservation commission hatched a scheme to connect Camp Hoover and Skyland. (Newsmen in a hurry had been making that trip on a combination of primitive "traces" in Model-A Fords.) Carson's inquiry as to whether Hoover would object brought a letter from Richey stating that, on the contrary, the President "thinks it would be a very good thing." The idea moved ahead but was shortly absorbed into the much larger concept of a Skyline Drive all along the Blue Ridge crest.

Horace Albright recently recalled a 1930 visit to Camp

Hoover during which the President initiated construction of the (previously proposed) Skyline Drive: "Mrs. Albright and I were there with other Interior Department bureau chiefs and their wives and the Secretary and his wife... Saturday he had a dinner in his home to discuss the budget... We ranged around his room — he didn't have any table — in order of our status in the department. I was the head of the youngest bureau, The National Park Service, so I was about the last one he would get to, you know."

Hoover claimed to be "the oldest man here" as to Interior Department service. Secretary Wilbur asked, "How do you figure that?" Hoover said he was in the Geological Survey before anyone else present. He'd been "a rodman or chainman or something," Albright remembered. But Dr. W. C. Mendenhall, Director of the Geological Survey, challenged the claim. "The President said, 'Well, let's compare. Let's get down to dates.' It turned out that Dr. Mendenhall was in there before him, so Mr. Hoover had to take second place on that — which he did graciously... All day we worked on that budget — until late afternoon when he told us to go fishing or do whatever we wanted to. Mainly we pitched horseshoes.

"Then we had another evening that was very fine... He announced that anybody who wanted to ride horseback should be out at the post at eight o'clock in the morning. Well, nobody was out there but me. The President then came along with his wife and Ted Joslin, one of his secretaries, and a Secret Service man — it wasn't Bill Starling. We rode up onto the summit — from the Rapidan to the Big Meadows area. Dead chestnut along as it was unkept, you know, but the trail was good because it was built for him.

"The President motioned me to come up alongside of him. He told me that these mountains were just made for a highway, and 'I think that everybody ought to have a chance to get the views from here. I think they're the greatest in the world, and I've been nearly everywhere in the world.' I pointed out that if they built a road there that's the end of his camp — because there'd be so many tourists they'd be flocking into it. He said, 'I'm not going to be President all the time, and my successor might not like this place, and besides I feel even if I were here the people should have this sensation that I have, this exhilaration, this experience that I have riding along here... I want you to consider undertaking a survey right away. Talk it over with Mr. Carson. Get a crew in here and see what you can do.' So that's where I got my instructions for this Skyline Drive. Right from the President's mouth, right up there where the road is now...

"It was a terribly dry year, and these people were impoverished... He asked for a congressional appropriation not only to relieve these farmers but to help other situations through the country. I don't remember how many million dollars it was, but he got it. His instructions to us were to get 'that survey going as fast as you can, and get your specifications for your highway, and then build it by force account if necessary, otherwise by contract, but insist that they use hand tools, the fresnoes and plows and scrapers of the farmers, and the farmers themselves.'... It was a welfare project. It was by Herbert Hoover. And it was before there was any 'New Deal.'... He pointed out there were places where you could ride the ridge and see both ways. You could look to the Piedmont and you could look to the Shenandoah Valley. Other places you could just look to one, and then you'd go round through a gap and you'd see the other side. He thought this was one of the greatest things about it. He noticed that in his own right, you see."

The highway system was only one facet of the Hoovers' impact. E. E. Chapman, chairman of Madison County's supervisors, thanked the President in 1929 for general advancement, in transportation, education, recreation, and economic growth, and this wider view was summed up in hyperbole by a present Madison leader who said, "Hoover's coming waked up Madison County for the first time since the landing at Jamestown!"

The over-all view was most completely expressed in "Hoover Day in Madison" (August 17, 1929), an all-out grassroots celebration that drew a crowd larger than the county's total population. This Big Day became such a legend that its anniversaries have sometimes been chosen for additional Madison fetes and ceremonies. It was conceived when the chamber of commerce, a small organization without employes, decided to invite the Hoovers to a party designed to thank them for noticing and helping the county. When, to the surprise of almost everyone, the Hoovers accepted, the chamber was not quite sure what to do next.

Time-honored procedure when in doubt is to appoint committees, and Dr. J. N. Clore, chamber president, did that.

Part of the crowd on "Hoover Day" in Madison County

Publicity ensued — and leaped onto front pages across the land. More personages were invited. Governor Harry F. Byrd (later Senator) announced he would arrive in a blimp. The local theatre manager boldly wrote Fox-Case Corporation, and was informed a crew with the latest news-reel equipment would be on hand. Maj. Long went into action and soon announced the Marine Band would play from 10 a.m. to 2 p.m.

A committee arranged to use the fairgrounds, and the chamber made this brave statement: "There's no telling how many people are coming, but we will be ready for them." Whereupon additional land adjoining the fairgrounds was volunteered. Someone thought to request officers from outside to help cope with traffic. The *Eagle* declared, "This is not only going to be Madison County's biggest day, but the biggest day in the United States of America or any of its possessions!"

The chamber's ambition grew: "While at first it was planned to serve dinner to the guests of the day, the militia, the bands and press representatives, the impression has gone forth that Madison County people will be hosts to all comers. There-

— with news reels being made. (Courtesy of J. B. Fray)

fore we are endeavoring to meet this duty. A great quantity of foodstuff has been promised — much more, in fact, than was at first estimated. In order to preserve our record for hospitality, more will be needed, and it is requested that every household will bring at least one well-filled basket containing more than the family will consume, with some to spare for visitors, and if possible two baskets, one entirely for the guest table..."

From the Blue Ridge crest to the woodlots of the Piedmont, men went out to shoot squirrels to go into fifty "old-time washpots" (about fifteen gallons each) of Brunswick stew. Cattle and pigs were readied for slaughter. Three hundred loaves of bread and five hundred chickens were ordered by the chamber. Five thousand tin cups were ordered for serving the squirrel stew.

Across six columns the *Eagle* of August 16 proclaimed: "MADISON COUNTY DAY AT HAND!"

Herbert Hoover, ruler of the greatest nation on earth, is to be the guest of his neighbors in the county, which he has

Speakers' stand on "Hoover Day" at Madison. (Courtesy of J. B. Fray)

honored by selecting it for his summer playground, where for the nonce he can put aside the great responsibilities and cares the American people have willed he should bear. Here he breathes the liberal mountain air, which Heine, the poet, said made men fit for service...

It is reported that people from a distance have been on the way to Madison all the week. They will be here from near and far. Many notables will be in the immense throng, who will help Madison County people to extend the glad hand to our chief Magistrate...

Representatives of the large press associations were here Monday making preparations to report the Day. A direct telegraph wire will run from the speakers' stand to Washington, so the speeches and happenings of the day can be disseminated instantaneously to all parts of the world. Many special and noted newspaper and magazine writers will be on hand for the sole purpose of telling the world about Madison County and the presence of President and Mrs. Hoover...

They seem to know about Madison County Day every-

where!

Madison leaders slept little that night. They had already done all they could — but they checked this and that to see if everything really was ready, and then they double-checked. Housewives had more reason to stay up late and rise again before dawn. Food is better when fresh, and dishes had to be packed for safe transportation. The Day came at last.

As early as 8 o'clock (the *Eagle* reported) automobiles began to roll into the grounds. Supervised by trained men from the motor vehicle department's constabulary, the parking of the several thousand cars was so well done that there was not a single hitch... There was a steady stream of automobiles coming from both directions until 10:30 o'clock, when the traffic began to gradually lessen in volume, but continued until the arrival of the Presidential party...

The first big event of the day was the arrival of Gov. Harry Flood Byrd in the Army blimp. The big airship drew the attention of the multitude soon after 10 o'clock as its nose appeared over the treetops coming from the south. It circled gracefully overhead and came down gently on the side of the hill back of the exhibition building...

Meantime the two bands had arrived and taken their places in the bandstands and were alternately filling the air with melody; a detachment of the Richmond Light Infantry Blues and 14 members of the Monticello Guard, the latter wearing their colonial uniforms, had arrived. The blimp, after the governor and party had disembarked, arose and circled and circled the grounds, each time making a wider circle for the purpose of giving all for miles around a glimpse...

At 11:30 o'clock the battery positioned in the hollow at the eastern edge of the fairgrounds began to speak, and a lusty voice yelled, "Here he comes!" meaning Mr. Hoover. The cry was taken up by thousands of throats as the guns fired the Presidential salute of 21 guns... As Mr. and Mrs. Hoover alighted, they were received by Dr. J. N. Clore... who had associated with him prominent countymen and ladies to act as a reception committee, for the most part heads of the various committees. The band played "Hail to the Chief"... The great ovation was a warm-hearted welcome to Mr. and Mrs. Hoover —an earnest that they had come among friends when they chose to locate their mountain retreat in this county and in Virginia.

Mrs. Hoover wore a gray and black crepe dress of floral design. Her hat was black and of large type. The President and the Governor both wore black business suits and brown soft hats. Their apparel did not distinguish them from the other guests on the grounds...

J. B. Fray (now Madison County treasurer) was secretary of the chamber then. He remembers that the five thousand tin cups "ran out before we got well started serving from those fifty washpots of stew. Hoover had planned to stay just half an hour, but the crowd and our welcome impressed him so he passed the word through Col. Starling of the Secret Service that he'd stay for lunch. The guests had been roped off from the bigger crowd, so we could handle it okay. There was a fifty-pound ham on the President's table."

The way the *Eagle* eye saw it, "Mr. and Mrs. Hoover enjoyed the feast, eating as all the other guests and surrounded by a great crowd, feasting as they were. The Hoovers ate Madison County fried chicken, Madison County ham, Madison County pie, and Madison County cake. Mr. Hoover also expressed a desire for some of Tom Early's Madison County bar-becued beef. It was soon forthcoming and all the distinguished guests were served from the heaping platter by the President himself..."

Mr. Fray remembers there was food left over even after feeding "somewhere around 10,000 people," so much that "the surplus was taken in trucks to the Marines up at the camp — who sent back their thanks saying 'they were mighty good eats!'"

The *Eagle* printed in full the words of Dr. Clore, Rep. J. A. Garber, Gov. Byrd, President Hoover, and an afternoon address by Mr. Carson which thanked by name scores of those who had contributed to establishment of the President's camp and those who continued to work toward completion of Shenandoah National Park.

Hoover's brief address was dear to the people of Madison County and has been the source of quotations, notably about fishing and drawing refreshment from nature, which have circulated worldwide:

> Both Mrs. Hoover and I feel greatly honored by the general reception you have extended us today. It is a welcome as one of your neighbors and it is as a neighbor that I participate with you.
>
> In the early years of our republic, Virginia was the home of Presidents, and it would seem appropriate that with the changing years, the President should at least have a weekend camp in Virginia. There are other sound reasons why such a connection should be maintained between the Presidents and Virginia.
>
> The fact is that those strong Virginians who selected the site for our national capital were apparently impervious to heat and humidity or at least they were unaware of how much pavements and modern buildings can contribute to raise the temperature. But Virginia herself now offers the antidote in the wonderful mountains which you have dedicated to a national park and the access to it that you have provided by your newly improved roads.
>
> It has become a habit and a necessity for our government officials who have the major anxieties in national affairs, to seek some other place from which to conduct their work for prolonged periods in the summer time. But the press of public business and its execution in the national capital is so necessary

that we must face the fact that these periods must gradually be shortened.

Therefore, I have thought it appropriate to accept the hospitality of your citizens and your mountains for one or two days each week and thereby combine both relief and work without cost to either. And I have discovered that even the work of the government can be improved by leisurely discussions of its problems out under the trees where no bells or callers jar one's thoughts from the channels of urbanity.

You have demonstrated yourselves good hosts and good neighbors with that fine courtesy for which Virginia is known to the whole nation. I often think the test of good neighbors is whether one can always be sure when the family meets an emergency it can cheerfully borrow a half-dozen eggs or a few extra dishes.

In this emergency you have proved this sentiment of neighborliness by lending me a part of your park, by improving a road, by securing the fishing rights on a beautiful mountain stream and even providing me with fishing tackle. I, on my side, am glad to lend my services as a good neighbor to you by acting as a sort of signpost to the country of the fine reality of your proposed new national park.

I fear that the summer camp we have established on the Rapidan has the reputation of being devoted solely to fishing. That is not the case, for the fishing season lasts but a short time in the spring. It is a place for weekend rest — but fishing is an excuse and a valid reason of the widest range of usefulness for temporary retreat from our busy world.

In this case it is the excuse for return to the woods and streams with their retouch of the simpler life of the frontier from which every American springs. Moreover, I have learned that fishing has an important implication and even sounder foundation of such an excuse from the Presidential point of view. I find that many Presidents have joined the ranks of fishermen only after their inauguration as President, although I can claim over 45 years of apprenticeship — that is, in fishing, not the Presidency.

I have discovered the reason why Presidents take to fishing — the silent sport. Apparently the only opportunity for refreshment of one's soul and clarification of one's thoughts by solitude to Presidents lies through fishing. As I have said in another place, it is generally realized and accepted that prayer is the most personal of all human relationships. On such occasions as that men and women are entitled to be alone and undisturbed.

Next to prayer, fishing is the most personal relationship of man and of more importance than the fact itself, everybody concedes that the fish will not bite in the presence of the public. Fishing seems to be the sole avenue left to Presidents through which they may escape to their own thoughts and may live in their own imaginings and find relief from the pneumatic hammer of constant personal contacts, and refreshment of mind in the babble of rippling brooks.

Moreover, it is a constant reminder of the democracy of life, of humility and of human frailty — for all men are equal before fishes. And it is desirable that the President of the United States should be periodically reminded of this fundamental fact — that the forces of nature discriminate for no man.

But to become more serious, I wish again to thank you on behalf of Mrs. Hoover and myself for your generous and cordial welcome to Madison County. We hope to be good neighbors, and we know from experience already that you will be.

That afternoon the Hoovers opened their camp to visitors, and hundreds drove up to see it and its surroundings, the first such opportunity for most of them.

A woman from Madison, living in California, wrote the *Eagle* she had heard the program broadcast — "every word so clearly... What a Big Day it really was with all the nation listening in. I am so glad the Madison folks have an opportunity to know President Hoover."

IV

The President and the Prime Minister

A poll of the many who still remember the active years at Camp Hoover, yet never visited there, would show one mental picture leading all the rest. There would be two solemn men, the weight of public rsponsibility almost visible on their shoulders, and they would be sitting on rough logs in a forest beside a mountain stream, talking earnestly. Their names would be Herbert Hoover and Ramsay MacDonald, and, in the over-dramatic words so often repeated, they would be "conspiring to sink the world's navies."

When Prime Minister Ramsay MacDonald of Great Britain and his daughter Ishbel arrived at the White House on October 4, 1929, President Hoover did not wait for them to be ushered inside. He went out on the portico to greet them. And that was where, according to talk that may or may not have originated with actual witnesses, Hoover told MacDonald they would not be staying at the White House that night, nor even in the city of Washington. "We are driving to the Blue Ridge Mountains and my isolated camp," Hoover said.

The Prime Minister seemed startled. "But, Mr. President —I can't go to the mountains in this cutaway and striped trousers!"

Britain's Prime Minister Ramsay MacDonald, wearing a suit lent him by Hoover for camp living, poses with the President on the portico of the White House. (Library of Congress)

"Don't worry about that," Hoover answered.

Versions of the story vary, but apparently the visiting dignitaries' luggage was soon sorted, part of it to be left at the White House, part of it to be taken to the Rapidan. Apparently, too, the President lent MacDonald a suit for camp wear and Mrs. Hoover augmented Ishbel's wardrobe for the same purpose.

In recalling the MacDonald visit during the writing of his *Memoirs*, Hoover did not reveal when he first told the Prime Minister they would be conferring in the wilderness. He wrote: "Shortly after his arrival I motored him to the Rapidan camp, and during the ride had an opportunity to discuss freely the subjects I had in mind. He seemed receptive upon many of them. At one moment he queried, 'How would you express these matters to the public of the two countries?' I stated I would make a draft covering my ideas... Secretary Stimson did not think I would get far with most of these proposals, but I thought they would test MacDonald's views..." The principal subject was, not "sinking" exactly, but limitation of navies in order to stop the armaments race which was straining financial resources and threatening world peace.

World War I, while destroying German naval power, had greatly stimulated warship building by the United States, Britain and Japan. After the Armistice, each of these three nations found itself committed to burdensome programs of naval construction, and in an atmosphere of mutual and growing suspicion each was vying for supremacy. A Washington conference in the Harding Administration had, after ten weeks of discussion by representatives of the United States, Britain, Japan, France and Italy, adopted the Hughes plan which set a 5-5-3 naval ratio. This ratio, however, applied mostly to battleships, and since there was no limit on submarines or any craft under 10,000 tons, competition in building smaller vessels was actually being stimulated toward the tinder point.

It was in the stress of this armaments race that Hoover had developed his military policies. But they could not accomplish their purpose without the cooperation of other nations, particularly of Great Britain. Summarizing the background of his invitation to MacDonald, Hoover wrote:

> My policies in national defense and world disarmament had one simple objective. That was to insure freedom from war to the American people.

The size of naval and military forces required to insure our country against aggression rests partly upon our foreign policies and partly upon the relative strength of possible enemies. The American concept had always been for defense, not for aggression. Our defense required that we defend the whole Western Hemisphere. We needed to have such strength that European and Asiatic aggressors would not even look in this direction...

Manifestly, with great ocean moats between us and possible enemies, our principal military needs at this time were naval and air forces. With such assurance against foreign armies landing in this hemisphere, we would rely upon a small skeleton army capable of quick expansion.

Early in my administration, I put the question to the Navy and Army staffs: "Are our defenses strong enough to prevent a successful landing of foreign soldiers on the continental United States and ultimately on the Western Hemisphere?"

The staffs had replied "emphatically 'Yes,'" so he had tackled naval limitation as the primary opportunity to strengthen world peace. "We could deal with other nations for proportional reduction on navies, but could only persuade on armies," he pointed out. The United States Navy was second in size then. Britain and Japan were competing with us, and the meaningful question concerned relative strength. "It seemed to me simple common sense to see if we could not come to an

Prime Minister's Cabin. (NPS)

agreement to limit further expansion," Hoover explained, especially as the smaller vessels left out of the existing agreement made up almost three-quarters of total tonnage.

Coolidge had inspired a conference in 1927 for the purpose of extending limitation to cruisers, destroyers, submarines and other craft, but it had failed — largely because Britain had refused at that time to accept parity with the United States. Hoover had promptly taken up the problem and worked out fresh instructions to American diplomats. Under these instructions Ambassador Gibson made an appeal on April 22, 1929, to the League of Nations Committee on Disarmament. On May 30 Hoover proposed that a naval conference be held to extend limitation to all warships. He insisted, however, on thorough preparation — no conference unless there was advance agreement upon major principles by major powers.

The number-one key to advance agreement was MacDonald. Gen. Charles G. Dawes, ambassador to Britain, was asked to find out whether MacDonald would carry on preliminary discussions (through diplomatic channels) with Hoover himself, instead of working through committees of technicians as had become customary, and whether MacDonald would agree to keeping the Japanese informed about these discussions. The British leader would and did, and the discussions brought early agreement to extend the battleship formula of 5 for Britain, 5 for the U. S., and 3 for Japan to all craft except submarines.

But this was not enough to assure lasting stability, and further negotiations came repeatedly near the breaking point through activities of the British Admiralty (based on allegedly insoluble difficulties in assessing comparative power of different individual ships and in agreeing upon dates for adding new ships or retiring outmoded ones). MacDonald was not very good at figures, and the "old salt-sea dogs" of the Admiralty tangled him in technicalities.

As Hoover explained, "They were naturally suspicious that the 'two welfare workers' — MacDonald and myself — were in a conspiracy to injure 'that greatest safeguard of world peace and world stability,' the British Navy. I had no such difficulties. Admirals Pratt, Hepburn, and Jones genuinely supported what we were trying to do. They believed that it was the road to peace and that a limited, well-rounded Navy would be more efficient in defense of the Western Hemisphere. After five weeks of interminable negotiations through the State Department we were getting nowhere."

Trying to cut the confusion, Hoover sent a personal cable expressing disappointment and outlining the only basis America would accept, including all the necessary technical details spelled out for MacDonald's benefit. This cable apparently cleared the air, and on September 17, to further narrow the gap, Hoover dictated a long letter to MacDonald — then, to abide by diplomatic tradition, changed the pronouns and addressed it to the U. S. Secretary of State who forwarded it to Dawes for MacDonald to read. MacDonald interpreted the letter as it had been dictated. "What I take as a personal letter from your President to myself..." he wrote in starting his reply. On this newly personal basis, then, correspondence rapidly narrowed the differences until Hoover felt the whole problem could be settled in face-to-face talk.

Ishbel MacDonald's Cabin. (NPS)

He had two Rapidan cabins prepared (and even named) for the Prime Minister and for Ishbel, his daughter. "My immediate purpose in extending an invitation to Prime Minister MacDonald to visit the United States," he wrote, "was of course to settle the remaining questions as to the naval limitations. I, however, had in mind broader questions as to the relations between Britain and the United States... I felt that MacDonald's winning personality, the fact he represented the British Labor Party, and his oratorical abilities on a visit would prove beneficial to relations between the two countries."

Such was the situation as the President and the Prime Minister rode side by side toward the remote Rapidan. The camp party was to include only these two, plus Richey, Boone, Mrs. Hoover, Ishbel, and perhaps one man from the State Department.

There had been a possibly disrupting furor a few weeks before. An American naval expert, William Shearer, filed a suit in the New York Supreme Court against three major ship-building companies. Shearer acknowledged $50,000 in payments from the three firms for his work in organizing underground efforts against international agreements meant to reduce naval strength, efforts which had almost certainly contributed to failure of previous negotiations. He now demanded in court that the companies pay him large additional amounts. The situation was complicated, indicating Shearer himself might now favor reduction of armaments, but strongly suggesting the shipbuilders might again have secret machinations in process, designed to sabotage the new talks.

Learning of the suit, Hoover had issued a strong public statement, labeling such machinations "not a fitting thing" and expressing "determination that our present international negotiations shall not be interfered with by any such activities ... or methods." Perhaps the already-prepared but last-minute-disclosed shift of the talks to the Rapidan was partly a defense against interference.

The *Eagle* eye did not pretend to focus on national and world affairs. What the Hoovers did in Madison County, if in any way unusual, was news, but what the President worried about there, or talked about with associates and guests, was normally not. Thus, the weekly had been ignoring the downward slide of stocks which had started early in September and was continuing toward the frightening crash of late October, ignoring also the loud accusations that certain Senators used liquor flasks at dinners given by Wall Street leaders, and not mentioning either the loud public noise of other Senators demanding why Hoover's new Farm Board was not using its $500 million appropriation quickly to make agriculture prosperous.

The paper had come out on October 3 with no mention of MacDonald's trip to America, and though millions of words were printed or broadcast on that subject throughout the

world during the next week the *Eagle* of October 11 had its
report under a headline smaller than that announcing the
Madison County Fair or the "Whitlock-Deam Wedding Bells".

President Herbert Hoover entertained Premier Ramsay
MacDonald, of England, over Sunday at his lodge. They arrived Saturday afternoon, accompanied by a distinguished party.
About nightfall Mrs. Hoover, driving her own car and accompanied by Lady Ishbel MacDonald, the premier's daughter who
came with her father to this country, and her traveling companion, had a near-accident after passing Criglersville. A wheel
of her car slipped off a culvert, but Secret Service men soon
lifted the car back on the road.

There were flurries of snow at the camp Saturday night,
but Sunday was an ideal day. The guests of the President and
Mrs. Hoover had opportunity to inspect the camp and pro-
nounced it a charming retreat.

After their return to Washington, it was announced that
while in Madison the distinguished men had discussed momen-
tous questions affecting the two countries and the world as
well. "We have frankly reviewed all questions that might give
rise to friction between our peoples," the announcement said.
"Gratifying progress has been made and the conversations are
continuing."

Outdoor fireplace and bench logs—where the President and Prime Minister
sat for some of their discussions, while the world wondered. (Herbert Hoover
Presidential Library)

The President and Premier did much of their serious talking sitting on a log overlooking the trout pond. They equally enjoyed the great outdoors.

The first tangible result of the conversations between these two men was the announcement of invitations to Japan, France and Italy to join the American and British governments in a conference in January in London to limit their sea power as a step toward world peace.

Two columns wide above the short, one-column news report, the *Eagle* printed something, however, which its publisher considered important enough to clip and send to Richey as it "might interest the President." It was entitled, "IN THE WHITE HOUSE OF MADISON COUNTY":

> MacDonald and Herbert Hoover, for the sake of peace they swore
> That the scenes of death and carnage must cease for ever more.
> Down in Old Virginia they talked as man to man
> To solve the world-wide problem on the banks of the Rapidan.
> And where could these men work better than beneath Virginia skies,
> Away from the maddened throng of men and the crowd of eager eyes?
> For Virginia is the cradle where Woodrow had his birth,
> And died for the mighty problem, "Peace, Good Will on Earth."
>   —J. S. DeJarnette
>   Staunton, Virginia

When all the vast wordage published outside Madison County at the time is boiled down, it is evident the bigger papers did not do significantly better than the *Eagle*. There is still no clear and direct picture of the discussions themselves, nor of the visitors' enjoyment of the wild Blue Ridge. What were the actual attitudes of the principals? What did the Prime Minister do when not talking with Hoover? What occupied Ishbel's time?

Admiral Boone remembers they did look around, inspecting the camp. "I don't recall Prime Minister MacDonald fishing, but I'm not sure he didn't give it a try. He and President Hoover went out along the stream together once, probably more than once. Ishbel went riding with Mrs. Hoover, and I recall clearly she pitched horseshoes with Richey and me for a time." While Boone expressed no opinion as to whether the talks were more successful in the wilderness than they would have been in Washington, he said, "The President and apparently the Prime Minister were more relaxed, more informal, than could have been expected in other surroundings. And the President, at least, could work better on such crucial, infinitely complicated matters under the relaxing conditions of camp."

According to Hoover's *Memoirs*, he did what he had told MacDonald he would, extend "some memoranda I had already prepared into the sort of statement we might make. Its purpose was largely to reduce the discussion to definite points."

There is evidence he was alone for some time shortly after reaching camp, carefully considering the preliminary once-over the subjects had been given in the car en route, preparing the draft, perhaps revising and re-revising as was his habit — while MacDonald was apparently catching a nap after his long journey. The Hoover draft — an extraordinary, dream-type document projecting the greatest reasonably possible success of discussions which the two men had only just begun — was not released in those years. It is included here in its entirety because the Camp Hoover story would lack completeness and depth without its somewhat complex but intriguingly important revelations:

> In the field of reduction of international friction we have examined the broad problems of naval reduction and limitation. We have further examined the question of limitation upon construction of military bases and we have examined the question usually referred to under the heading of "freedom of the seas."
>
> We have engaged in an examination of the broad questions of reinforcing the peace of the world. The situation in the world has been importantly altered in consequence of the Pact of Paris. The declaration of that pact, "that the world has renounced war as an instrument of national policy," and its undertaking that settlement or solution of disputes and conflicts of whatever origin shall never be sought except by pacific means, re-orients all problems of peace.

> ### I
>
> In the furtherance of practical application of these ideas, we have examined the possibility of the extension of the Pact of Paris to strengthen measures against the outbreak of war and

to reinforce the machinery of pacific settlement of controversies.

We are united in the feeling that an advance step could be taken in development of pacific means for the settlement of controversies if an article, to be called "Article 3," could be added to the Pact of Paris to the effect that, in event of any controversy in which satisfactory settlement is not made by direct negotiation or agreed reference to arbitration or judicial decision, such controversy shall be investigated by a commission to be selected by the parties to the controversy, upon which commission the parties shall be represented together with impartial members; this commission to examine all the facts concerning the controversy, to endeavor to conciliate the difficulties and to publish the facts; that suggestion of the desirability of such action by nations strangers to the controversy would not be considered an unfriendly act.

The state of peace is recognized as normal by the Pact of Paris, and war is outlawed. All nations have a legitimate interest in the preservation of peace, and all are injured by a breach of peace.

The United States, in numerous treaties of conciliation with the leading powers of Europe, in treaties with the Pan American nations, in its adhesion to the Hague treaties, has already accepted these principles. The Covenant of the League of Nations provides that the Council of the League shall make such inquiry among its members. The principles of this suggestion, therefore, have been widely agreed to by the nations of the world.

This proposal differentiates itself from the older agreements in that it would extend the number of nations adhering to these ideas; it undertakes to secure action by initiative of the parties to the controversy themselves; to secure to each nation the right to have the facts determined and an appeal to public opinion, and to arouse world opinion and world conscience that the facts shall be determined.

II

One of the primary necessities of the world for the maintenance of peace is the elimination of the frictions which arise from competitive armament and the further necessity to reduce armament as economic relief to the peoples of the world. The negotiations which have taken place between the United States and Great Britain have been based upon a desire on both sides to find solutions to their peculiar problems which have hitherto stood in the way of world agreement on this question.

The negotiations which have taken place during the past three months have resulted in such an approximation of views as has warranted the calling of a conference of the leading naval powers in the belief that at such a conference all views can be reconciled. (Between ourselves we have agreed upon parity, category by category, as a great instrument for removing the competition between us.) All the reconsideration of capital ship replacement programs provided in the Washington Arms Treaty, the limitation and reduction in the categories of cruisers, destroyers, and submarines, yield strong hope of final agreement, and it has been agreed that we shall continue to mutually examine these questions involved prior to the conference. And we shall continue to exchange views upon questions and concurrently discuss these views with the other naval powers.

III

With further view to reducing friction and minimizing the possibility of conflicts, we believe that we should agree that Great Britain should not establish new or maintain fortified military bases in the Western Hemisphere, such area to be defined as that portion of the globe lying west of, say, the 25° meridian to the 180° meridian, or thereabouts; and that the United States on the other hand should not establish or maintain military bases in the Eastern Hemisphere, except so far as that provided in the Pacific treaties of 1922 — the Eastern Hemisphere for this purpose to be defined as that area of the globe lying east of the 25° meridian to the 180° meridian.

IV

We recognize that one of the most troublesome questions in international relations is that of freedom of the seas. Not only does this subject arouse fear and stimulate naval preparation, but it is one of the pregnant causes of expansion of the area of war once it may have broken out, by dragging other nations in as the result of controversies with belligerents.

Misunderstandings arising out of these questions have been the greatest cause of controversies in the past between our two countries. We have resolved therefore that we will examine this question fully and frankly.

The President proposes, and he hopes the American people will support the proposal, that food ships should be declared free from interference during times of war, and thus remove starvation of women and children from the weapons of warfare. That would reduce the necessity for naval arms in protection of avenues of food supplies. Such a proposal goes wider than the rights of neutrals in times of war and would protect from interference all vessels solely laden with food supplies in the same fashion that we now immunize hospital and medical supplies.

The bannered reports in the world press — about the Rapidan talks promoting world peace in the presence of only "those green-robed senators of mighty woods" — were as much padded speculation as facts, almost as short of real information as the popular talk about "sinking the world's navies."

In early October, with snow flurries on Saturday followed by a bright Sunday and Monday, the air was almost certainly chilly except briefly just after noon. The leaves of the tulip trees and of birches along the streams would have been taking on their autumn yellows, while the maples would have been hinting of brilliant reds to come. The large fireplaces in the cabins would have been blazing and crackling with chestnut wood. Whether the two world leaders talked mostly inside by a warm fire, or sitting on logs by the outdoor fireplace where newspaper pictures were posed, or on other logs near some "trout pond" as the *Eagle* said, or while walking in the woods or along the stream, perhaps does not matter. The Camp Hoover atmosphere would have affected them everywhere while also absorbing into itself, for those who might come later to this historic place, overtones of world destiny outlasting the specific men who faced the great issues there.

Hoover wrote in his *Memoirs* that he made one other proposal verbally to MacDonald "which hitherto has not been made public. I suggested that the British consider selling to us Bermuda, British Honduras, and the island of Trinidad. I told him I thought we could give them a credit upon the war debt which would go a long way to settle that issue. I explained that we were not interested in their West Indian possessions generally. I wanted Bermuda and Trinidad for defense purposes, and I wanted to have British Honduras as an item to use in trading with Mexico for the use of the mouth of the Colorado River so as possibly to cure certain frictions between Mexico and Guatemala.

"He did not rise to the idea at all. He even excluded British Honduras although, aside from officials, probably fewer than 1,000 Englishmen got a living out of it. I had a hunch he did not take the payment of the debt very seriously."

In regard to major subjects, Hoover reported (on subject I of the draft, Pact of Paris, or Kellogg Pact): "Mr. MacDonald toyed with the idea of a further article to the Kellogg Pact but finally ... concluded it would be objected to by the League of Nations as building up rival instrumentalities. In the view of both Secretary Stimson and myself, this was not the case as it was a strengthening of the League provisions and might free the League of many controversies. Moreover, it would include nations not in the League."

As to the principal problem (subject II in the draft, naval limitation): "On the 6th at Rapidan Camp we went down the creek and on a log threshed out the points as yet unsettled in the naval agreement. We felt Japan would go along, but we did not believe we could secure the agreement of France or Italy. While their naval strength was much inferior to the three major powers, they were engaged in a bitter naval competition with each other in which France was demanding an inferior fleet for Italy. We decided that, if they would not agree, we would make it a tripartite agreement between the United States, Britain, and Japan anyway."

As to British military bases in the Western Hemisphere (subject III), Hoover told MacDonald that improvement of such naval and air bases by Britain "might at any time become a live coal in the American mind." He had already proposed defining a pole-to-pole line down mid-Atlantic and mid-Pacific beyond which neither the United States nor Britain, on their respective sides, should expand air or naval bases. MacDonald said he would urge its acceptance upon the British Admiralty, and he did so by cable. Before leaving the U.S. he received an answer and reported to Hoover "with genuine regret" that they rejected it absolutely. Hoover felt that an opportunity to reassure the world was thus lost. His *Memoirs* contain this further comment: "However, the British made no additions to these bases for some years."

As to "freedom of the seas" (subject IV): Hoover found MacDonald sympathetic to immunizing food ships from military harm as was done for hospital ships. But after returning to England, MacDonald reported he could get nowhere with the plan. This reaction was not unexpected as Hoover realized "the British Admiralty's military vision was fixed on the idea that wars are won by starving people through blockade, and its primary argument for a big navy was protection of British food supplies." (A month later Hoover made public in an

Armistice Day address his hope of immunizing food ships, and, though it was welcomed by the press elsewhere, it was so violently opposed in Britain and Japan that it had to be abandoned.)

It might be said that these Rapidan talks, of which the world eagerly awaited solid news, resulted in four failures and only one success, but perhaps the one success outweighed the failures. On October 10, the President and the Prime Minister issued a joint statement:

> Our conversations have been largely confined to the mutual relations of the two countries in the light of the situation created by the signing of the Peace Pact. Therefore, in a new and reinforced sense the two governments not only declared that war between them is unthinkable... On the assumption that war between us is banished, and that conflicts between our military or naval forces cannot take place, these problems have changed their meaning and character and their solution, in ways satisfactory to both countries, has become possible.

Thus concluded the meeting that had made Camp Hoover, for a time, the news-center of the world — even while the Secret Service and the Marines kept reporters at a distance from the conversations they would have liked to overhear.

The naval limitation movement continued strongly into the London Naval Conference of January 1930. That conference clinched what historians recognized as "a great and possibly the last practical accomplishment toward disarmament" of the post-World War I era. Hoover considered it a real success as far as Britain, the United States and Japan were concerned — but France and Italy could not agree on their relative strengths and only partially accepted the final treaty.

The U.S. Senate procrastinated on the Naval Limitation Treaty throughout its regular 1930 session, so Hoover called a special session for July 7, presenting a potent case for prompt ratification. Naturally, he explained, there was opposition from those who believe unrestricted military strength was the objective of America. The same type minds in Britain and Japan also opposed the treaty. The American majority, however, wanted military strength held in conformity with the sole purpose of national defense. The only alternative to this treaty, the President declared, was competitive building of navies, with all its flow of suspicion, hate, ill will, and ultimate disaster. Experience showed, he insisted, that every limitation increased good will and confidence.

The depression was straining the finances of the United States (and the rest of the world), and he declared that if the treaty were not ratified our expanded fleet construction would take $500,000,000 in the next few years and our navy still would not reach parity with Britain's. The treaty would also save hugely in annual operation costs of our navy, funds which could go far in solving other problems.

The treaty was ratified on July 22, 1930, and upon signing it Hoover said:

With the ratification by the other governments the treaty will translate an emotion deep in the hearts of millions of men and women into a practical fact of government and international relations. It will renew again the faith of the world in

The hope of more certain peace.

Cartoon of the period by Bronstrup, depicting the President and the Prime Minister in conference at Camp Hoover. (Herbert Hoover Presidential Library)

the moral forces of good will and patient negotiation as against the blind forces of suspicion and competitive armament. It will secure the full defense of the United States. It will mark a further long step toward lifting the burden of militarism from the backs of mankind and speed the march forward of world peace. It will lay the foundations upon which further constructive reduction in world arms may be accomplished in the future...

World spotlights did not again shine so searchingly upon the Rapidan, though Camp Hoover was yet to be the source of major news and human-interest stories that would not be forgotten. But even if the camp were never to be more than a peace symbol, it had its place in world history.

V

The Possum-Boy and the Mountain School

Human-interest writers exercised imagination as freely over the opossum-carrying barefoot boy who "caused" the Hoover School as the world-affairs pundits did over the Hoover-MacDonald talks. There was agreement on but one simple sequence of facts: A mountain boy appeared with an opossum at Camp Hoover on August 10, 1929, the President's fifty-fifth birthday. Six months later a school for Blue Ridge children opened, with the possum-boy among the pupils, in a brand-new building near the clearing where the airplane dropped Presidential mail.

The first printed version of the possum story had the boy — Ray Burraker, or Ray McKinley, or William McKinley Buraker called Bill —-slipping past both the Marines and the Secret Service. He appeared before Hoover unannounced and presented the opossum, after which there was a conversation revealing the lack of a school, a deficiency Hoover immediately decided to eliminate.

But, as if someone had objected to the implication the President was poorly guarded, a different version took over:

"Young man, why aren't you in Sunday school?" This question by Mrs. Hoover was directed with mock severity toward an 11-year-old Blue Ridge mountain boy. The tousle-headed youth, carrying a fat baby possum in a cage fashioned of a soap box and chicken wire, was trudging near the Hoover camp when spied by Mrs. Hoover's Sunday horseback riding party.

'I uster go t' Sunday school," replied the unabashed youngster, "but maw tol' me to take this yere coon down to the President fer his birthday."

One word led to another and eventually Mrs. Hoover took the boy in tow to camp where he met not only the President but such notables as Col. Lindbergh, Secretary of Agriculture Hyde, and Surgeon Gen. Cummings.

Mr. Hoover received the present with dignity until the visitor remarked: "My pappy said ef you wuz e-lected he'd climb a hickory tree." The President laughed heartily. However, the boy's father later amplified this by admitting he had "clumb" a tree, but it "warn't no hickory" but an oak tree,

White House opossum, perhaps the very one presented by the mountain boy to the President on August 10, 1929. (Library of Congress)

and that he "clumb it quicker'n a squirrel" because he was "so tickled Hoover got elected."

Mr. Hoover declined to eat the possum but turned it over to his son Allan as a camp pet. However, he gave the mountain lad a crisp new $5 bill in exchange for his gift.

The boy, whose name is Ray McKinley or Ray Burracker (there seems to be some doubt which, the family saying they adopted McKinley because the other was "too hard" to say) became quite chummy with the Chief Executive. Together they looked over the Sunday rotogravure sections, though Ray couldn't read or write, and worked out several puzzles which Mr. Hoover gave the boy.

There is still a question if Ray had previously heard of Col. Lindbergh. One correspondent reported that Ray didn't seem to know the name, but another declared that when introduced to Lindbergh the boy remarked, "Why, it's Lindy!"

Though Ray had never gone to school his "pappy" could read and write, holds prayer meetings in his weather-beaten log cabin 3,500 feet above the Rapidan, and the family daily see an airmail plane fly overhead. The boy confided to the President that he was "sorta glad" he was elected. Ray is one of eight brothers and sisters. The sort of upper half-story of his three-room house is reached by an outside stairway of rough-hewn timber, and his father once tore up a new dress belonging to one of his daughters because it wasn't "decent."

When asked if he knew any of the Hill Billy songs Ray was properly indignant. He knows them all. For the President's benefit he sang "I'll Meet You Up There in the Morning." But when invited to remain for dinner the lad insisted that he had "et." After saying good-by Ray wended his way up the mountain, kicking up little spurts of dust with his bare feet in ecstasy of having met the "big folks."

With true business instinct, Ray several days later vainly tried to sell the President two more raccoons. Which adds some basis to the rumor that Ray's meeting with the President was a pre-arranged affair, inspired by newspapermen.

This rehash of mythology, into which a few handy facts had been absorbed, circulated widely despite obvious errors including the author's confusion of opossum and raccoon — ignorance which even the most illiterate mountain lad would scorn whether he knew Lindy or not. Variations were played and replayed. The political preference of the boy's father shifted: "My pappy bet in favor of Al Smith and had to climb the tree t'pay off the bet." *The Literary Digest,* following a hint in the New York *Telegram,* went so far as to credit (or blame) Mark Sullivan, who had been horseback riding with Mrs. Hoover and Richey, for pre-arranging the possum presentation.

The truth can become quickly elusive, some would even say irrelevant. To most newspapermen the mountain folk meant fun, not fact. Reporters relished such oddities as the old mountain man who discovered the first Marine bivouac on the Rapidan and rushed home to report, "The's a gen'r'l an' a hundred sub-Marines down thar!"

But the Hoovers enjoyed their neighbors differently. Long before the President's birthday, Mrs. Hoover and friends while

A Blue Ridge Mountain home. (NPS)

riding had become acquainted with several families. At camp there had been discussions of these unusual people, their origins, way of life and current needs. Mr. Hoover had expressed interest in them, even to associates in Washington, and it is not unlikely the school was already taking shape in his mind.

As to the opossum episode itself, evidence favors a version which was never published. Boone, the President's physician, was riding alone one day between camp and Big Meadows on the range-crest when he spotted a home he had not seen before. A boy was leaning on the fence, one foot up on a rail. Boone called greetings but heard no answer. Reining in his horse, he asked, "You live here?"

The boy, wearing coarse blue pants and shirt but no shoes, appeared to nod, or maybe only lowered his glance.

"Your name?"

The boy finally spoke. "Buraker."

"Do you have a school around here?"

"Nope."

"Got a church?"

"Yup. This here house."

"Got a preacher?"

"Pop."

"What does he preach about?"

The boy puzzled over this question and finally said, "About two hours, I reckon."

Boone had read *The Little Shepherd of Kingdom Come* (by John Fox, Jr.) and saw the situation clearly. Knowing how much the Hoovers loved children, he rode back to camp and told them about the Buraker boy. The President said, "Tell that boy if he will bring me an opossum down here I'll give him five dollars."

Boone delivered the message, but weekends passed without results. The President's birthday arrived, and Boone rode up again. The boy was leaning against the fence, but this time he hailed the doctor first. "Got possum," he said.

"Good — but you have to take it down to the President."

The boy held back, but Boone offered to let him ride the horse, which proved a powerful inducement. Boone walked, carrying the opossum tied in an old gunny sack.

The boy did not shed his shyness at camp, and the conversations were slight. The opossum was delivered, however, and the five dollars paid. Lindbergh was present, and President Hoover told the boy, "This is Colonel Lindbergh."

"Never heerd o' him."

"He's the young man who flew alone across the ocean."

The boy was interested but hardly responsive.

Lindbergh went around back of a tree and Boone followed and talked with him. "That's the best news I ever heard — finest thing ever happened to me," Lindbergh said, "— meeting someone who never heard of me."

President Hoover extended an invitation to dinner, but the boy declined in acute shyness.

"This is my birthday," the President said, persuading. "There's a big cake."

"Had m' dinner."

Good-bys were said. The opossum was given to the valet, who was to make a cage for it. Later, the boy was observed eating with the valet in the "galley" back of the Mess Hall. He was even persuaded to accept a piece of the big cake and take other pieces home to family members.

After receiving some education in the school for which he helped plant the seed, Ray Buraker, the possum-boy, was invited to the White House. He had his tonsils out at the Navy hospital and was taken sightseeing by "Boots" Miller, Mrs. Hoover's chauffeur, who had been given twenty dollars to spend on him. Today he lives across the Potomac River from

Washington.

"But the Hoover School," Admiral Boone said, "—establishment of that school was the real story. And the wonderful way Christine Vest ran it and helped the mountain people."

The Madison County *Eagle* did not mention the possumboy until after the legend had been built up, and then only incidentally. Here is the Hoover item of August 16, 1929 (which Boone discounts as to supervision of the dinner and as to the President's physical participation in dam building):

Mr. Hoover's 55th birthday was observed in a quiet way. Mrs. Hoover and Mrs. Lindbergh supervised the dinner which consisted principally of the President's favorite dishes. He himself had whetted his appetite by supervising and assisting in making more dams for trout pools. The stream has been stocked with thousands of trout since the preserve was established, and some of them have grown large and venturesome. Not realizing they cannot live in water of a higher temperature than at the lodge, they swim downstream and die. A number have been lost in this way.

When, with its September 6 issue, the *Eagle* sighted in on the possible school, it demonstrated the same thorough alertness shown when the camp was being established:

President Hoover has decided to initiate a move looking to the education of mountain children living in the sparsely settled region surrounding his fishing camp... For some time Mr. Hoover has been impressed with the lack of advantages for children in this section, and Sunday he asked "Pa" Buraker to visit him. Plans for the school were discussed as the two, one the President of the United States and the other a rugged mountaineer, sat beneath the trees which shade the fishing camp.

Buraker agreed to head a committee of local citizens, while the President promised to head a national committee to raise funds for the purpose. It is expected that only $1,200 will be needed to erect the school building. There are five families in the immediate neighborhood, including the Buraker family which has five children of school age.

The *Eagle*, during the next five months, carried many long articles related to the school, elaborating these high points:

September 13 - Hoover sets up a $1,200 fund to speed establishment of a school for mountain children.

The Herbert Hoover Mountain School. (NPS)

September 20 - School fund increased to $2,000. State and county authorities heed public talk resulting from publicity and start studying the situation, with preliminary indications number of children justifies the operation... Hoover gives Mr. Buraker $50, presumably to obtain educational supplies.

September 27 - School plan advancing. Hoover to underwrite all costs. Virginia department of education and Madison County board surveying site and designing building.

October 11 - School construction starts, county school board having formally negotiated the job with assistance from state.

December 13 - Miss Ruth Fesler of White House staff and Miss Christine Vest, who may be named teacher of the Hoover Mountain School, are inspecting the Fairfax (Virginia) school for ideas and procedures. The new school above the President's camp will be furnished according to the latest approved plans of the Virginia education department.

February 7, 1930 — Miss Vest officially appointed, now conferring with Mrs. Hoover.

February 14 - Miss Vest arrives. School house is a model building of its kind — classroom, living room, kitchen, bedroom

Men who constructed the Hoover school pose on the building's steps. Among them are John Weakley, who was the school's nearest neighbor (bottom right with cane), Lester Weakley (middle row, second from left), June Weakley (middle row, second from right), Bealy Hurt (top row against right edge of door), and near center with high boots, probably E. F. Hart, supervisor of construction. (Courtesy of Capt. Lou K. Witcofski)

and bath on the lower floor, and two dormer rooms, two large fireplaces with stone chimneys, running water from a mountain spring... Construction was supervised by E. F. Hart representing the state board.

February 21 - Expected school opening delayed. Newsmen and photographers, here from hundreds of miles, wander off to look at scenery and mountain homes. Children arrive and find cameras. They are very careful not to break the strange instruments — and very careful not to injure the plate film as they remove this queer material from the holders for close examination, then, like good children, replace it exactly as they found it.

An Associated Press dispatch from Richmond quoted Raymond V. Long, supervisor of Virginia school buildings, as stating he had made many improvements in the design using ideas from the Hoovers. Cost of construction and furnishing had thus risen from the first estimate of $1,200 to over $8,000 despite donation of much equipment. Special features not usually provided in rural schools included electric lights, wall sockets for electric irons, radio and refrigerator, linoleum for the class-room and woolen rugs for other floors, extra bedrooms for guests or for emergencies such as illness in a mountain family whose home might lack comforts.

Clearly, the school was to be more than just a school, the teacher more than just a teacher. An information sheet issued by the President's office (but "not to be regarded as a White House statement") said the building "will be a gathering place for the mountain folk ... their contact with the outside world." Further, that the construction had employed mountain men so as to give them "an experience which would enable them to make their own home more comfortable by changes and additions suggested by the work they did on the school building."

Christine Vest, age 25, had appropriate qualifications. Born in the hills of Kentucky, she graduated from Berea College nearby, attended Columbia University, then taught mountain children in her home state. The Berea College president had called her when he received one of the Hoover letters asking recommendations, and she had agreed to having her name entered, though "without any real expectation of being selected from among all those who would be competing."

Weeks later she was invited for an interview (all expenses paid). She still vividly remembers being met by Miss Fesler and conducted to a third floor sitting room in the White House. "Mrs. Hoover came in soon, and we sat and talked and drank tea. Mrs. Hoover was wonderful — I came to admire both Mr. and Mrs. Hoover, and though people often ask me if I wasn't nervous about meeting them, or while with them, I really never was. They were so tolerant and thoughtfully concerned with others. As Dr. Ray Lyman Wilbur said at the memorial service for Mrs. Hoover, she 'could deal as understandingly and sympathetically with a gardener as with the head of a world conference. There is no finer example of how to live than was given us by Lou Henry Hoover.' I felt that, and I believe it completely to this day."

Christine was accompanied to the Hoover School on February 14 by Ruth Fesler (now Mrs. Robert L. Lipman), Mrs. Hoover's secretary, and Sue Dyer, a Hoover family friend. They arrived after dark. "Some men and boys had waited for me," she said, "and I wish you might have seen the eager anticipation in their eyes. They had big fires going, and we needed them... The second morning we awoke to find snow on the ground and the thermometer at nine degrees below zero. Water pipes were frozen... My guests left the third day — but already I was becoming fond of the mountain people. I was never afraid of them. I worked, the men worked, and the neighbors worked getting ready for the opening day."

In arranging the classroom, one mountain man picked up the geographic globe and said abruptly, "Miss Vest, do you believe the world is round?" "Yes," she said firmly. "Indeed I don't," he said even more firmly. "The Bible speaks of the four corners of the earth — and how can you get four corners out of this?"

Still only partly aware of what faced her in the Blue Ridge, Christine was plagued by reporters, often at inconvenient times. One reporter could not get any response at the front door so tried the back. She was house-cleaning and had on an old wrap-around apron and a rough scarf to protect her hair. He asked if the teacher was in, and she told him if he would wait out front she would try to find Miss Vest. She removed the disguising apron and scarf, went to the front door and invited him in. Many questions and answers later, he asked, "Are you the same person I met at the back door?" She said yes, and both had a good laugh. When she read the story he had written she found these words at its end, "And she has a sense of humor too!"

The opening day was February 24. Time flew so fast that morning, with so much yet to do, Christine was caught not yet ready when "all the people of the mountainside came up the slope." There were boys in overalls and sweaters, hair newly cut as if a bowl had been put over each head and the scissors snipped around the edge, faces glistening in the crisp air, probably scrubbed with homemade soap. There were girls in their best, regardless of age, hair tucked in a hard knot on the backs of their necks. The rosy cheeks were not entirely from the crisp air, Christine noticed. Remote as the place was, rouge had made its way up long before the Hoovers. And there were parents with stolid, yet curious faces, many carrying babies or leading children too small to walk alone.

Thirty-five reporters and photographers, representing Associated Press, Pathe, Paramount, United Press and others gave the impression the school opening was a spectacle staged for their benefit. And the mountain people, probably unconsciously cooperated more with the newsmen than with the teacher. Lights were being snapped on and off, water faucets

In class, Ray Buracker at front desk, teacher, Christine Vest, standing near center.

Patriarch of the district, Martin Jackson Buracker, 72, grandfather of Ray.

Youngest pupil, Virginia Buracker.
(Reproduced from old newspapers)

being turned on, maps were being pulled down and let flip up, the new books were being opened, and even the globe was whirling madly around. These people had never seen such things before. Christine concluded little could be done that day except talk and take the roll —and ask the children to return the next morning.

The United Press report stressed the "backwoods" situation "where poverty and ignorance go hand in hand" and focused on Ray Buraker, the possum-boy, "who went without breakfast so he could arrive first and raise the American flag in front of the brown and green school." Then it spotlighted relatives. "The boy's 71-year-old grandmother, Mart Buraker's wife, put on a faded blue sunbonnet, took her cane in hand and struggled over two miles of muddy mountain trail to the schoolhouse. Old Mart himself was there, a venerable patriarch with flowing white beard, feeling 'right smart bad' because the President did not come... Five-year-old Virginia Buraker wore a dress Mrs. Hoover had sent her... Celia Buraker, 11, wore an orange hat with morning glory trimmings, vintage of about 1905, probably handed down through the family for years... The Burakers seemed all over the place. Mrs. Mart, weary from her tramp and resting in front of the fireplace, counted eight grandchildren among pupils..."

The Associated Press could not resist datelining its dispatch "Dark Hollow, Va." — with some excuse as several pupils had walked from a location of that name, though the school itself was high on a ridge with a view of scenic peaks and the distant Piedmont Plain. The AP's lead paragraph was, "Book learning came to Dark Hollow today to join mountain lore." Its second, "The youngsters were to begin the magic trail of the printed word, and they came early with wonder-filled eyes."

Various rotogravure sections featured the Hoover Mountain School from February through July (that first session lasted until August 1). Photographers finally caught Mrs. Hoover with the pupils and teacher but never did manage to show the President there.

Extensive publicity brought many gifts, both before and after opening day. A large school-equipment company had donated the adjustable steel desks with space under the seats for the books and pads and pencils of the students. Charles Scribner's Sons, publishers, sent boxes of books. A Connecticut stationer wrote the President offering as many pencils free as could be used (but Richey informed him the school was already abundantly supplied). There was a surplus too in offers of Bibles — from individuals as well as from religious organizations. An Ohio nurseryman wanted to furnish "a respectable Bible to each family in the district, also to each pupil who can read intelligently or who may learn so to read."

There was a piano for a time, contributed by Richey, but Christine did not play and the mountain people, though fond of singing, were not familiar with pianos and showed little interest. Lou Witcofski sometimes brought the mail from the Marine Camp in the evenings and gave the piano a workout, but there are reasons to believe his interest was even stronger in the teacher than in music.

Hoover school class ready for excursion to the county fair. Miss Vest and a Madison official at back, left, (Jameson photo)

The school had unusual problems. "The Buraker family sent six beginners, ranging in age from five to fourteen," Christine Vest Witcofski said, remembering. "Reda, Pauline and Ray, who were above ten, wouldn't be interested in doing what five-year-old Virginia would..."

She had to work out her own groupings with little resemblance to the usual grades. At first there were three groups — those few who had been to school somewhere before and, luckily, were near the same age; those who were quite grown up but had never been to school; and the more or less typical beginners. But further divisions appeared until there were six groups, and in addition she was giving time to each child as partly in a category by himself. The classroom would hold thirty and sometimes was almost full, but the average was nearer twenty. When deep snow fell and blizzards blew, attendance dropped way down. Some children had five miles to walk, but even so they were reluctant to miss a day. The little ones sometimes arrived shivering, but in the heat from the school fires they quickly brightened.

There were never any discipline problems and seldom a lack of interest. Circumstances proved such that the children read into Christine whatever quality they most admired, even if her rating in the desired quality seemed low to her. When that happened, she simply had to become what they wanted and needed. One example: The Hoovers got Christine a four-year-old horse which was quite frisky. She was afraid of it at first, and when it reared almost to the point of falling backward she thought she would never ride it again. But then she heard a child commenting, " 'Deed, Miss Vest ain't afraid 'o nothin'!" — and knew she had to master the frisky beast no matter what the struggle involved.

Her main objective was to help the children help themselves. Regular state textbooks were used as the children would be entering the state school system when their families moved out to clear the national park. She tried to introduce life as it was lived outside the mountains, including automobiles and cities, modern homes and stores. She taught arithmetic as eggs and chickens, which they already knew, then as money and merchandise, which most of them did not. She taught measuring. "Yes," she said, "I had girls and boys fifteen and sixteen years old who had never measured anything with a ruler or yardstick!" They measured wood, cloth, the school room and furniture — then boards and sawed them up and made things of them with tools they had never seen before.

She taught 16-year-old girls how to order from a catalog, a procedure that interested them greatly and involved all three basic subjects, reading, writing and number work. Sometimes there was money, and an order was actually sent off. Mrs. Hoover contributed a sewing machine, and the older girls learned to use it. Christine had two patterns (a six-year-old

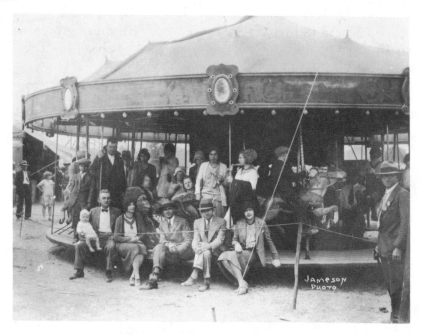

The school children enjoy the merry-go-round. (Jameson photo)

and a number 36) which soon guided cutting cloth for dresses. The sewing machine did a real service in alterations and in mending torn clothing. The girls also learned to read simple recipes, to measure the ingredients and to cook in ways other than frying, which had been an almost universal mountain habit.

Boys and girls alike were taught to write letters to their kin living elsewhere, to sweethearts, to Sears Roebuck. They became familiar with newspapers, first intrigued by their own pictures in them, later learning to find Moon Mullins in the comic sections. Magazines and books other than texts were introduced. Students varied in ability as elsewhere, but in the 8-12 age group quite a few advanced four grades in three years.

School closed at 3:30, but Christine's work was never done. Adults would be wanting letters read or written, perhaps to a daughter who had married and moved away. Or they came requesting newspapers to paper the walls of their houses. Or a baby was sick —and did the teacher, please, have any castor oil? "After supper," Christine said, "the lovely living room with rug on the floor, cheery fire in the big fireplace, and a radio, was an invitation to all. Grown-ups gathered for many happy evenings, and there was teaching even at 6:45 when

Lowell Thomas came on the air, because he told of places and things they had never heard of and wanted to have explained."

Finding out the children really were learning to read and write, a few fathers would not be outdone and came in the evenings to do likewise. One man learned with great rapidity. "I'll never forget the look of joy on his face," Christine said, "when he learned how to write all the names of his large family on the blackboard." Soon he was reading almost everything, as well as writing letters and doing additions and subtractions of money. Then he registered and became a voter for the first time in his life.

The classroom was soon being used on Sunday mornings for religious instruction, with attendance as high as fifty. Christine taught Sunday school, but the services, without denominational affiliation, were a community function, not actually her responsibility. Occasionally, guests of the Hoovers would attend. George Buraker, the possum-boy's father, became the "preacher," and scripture-quoting and hymn-singing were obviously enjoyed by the mountain folk, young and old.

Christine invited mountain girls to live with her for a time, and increasingly girls came for warm baths in the privacy of the school's bathroom. "It wasn't always just for the girls' sakes I invited them," she said. "That place could be scary for a person alone at night, especially when there was mist or snow with those blight-killed, ghosty chestnut trees dimly showing through, and strange sounds out in the wilderness. But I never confessed this reason then."

Christine wore her hair bobbed. The question arose whether short hair was a sin for girls — she was often asked whether this or that was a sin, but usually avoided giving a definite answer. Soon the girls began appearing with bobbed hair. She insists she never cut any girl's hair — but she did give haircuts to boys, while they sat on a special stump in the school's back yard.

The families generally did not own the land they lived on, most of which belonged to the Graves family. They looked after Graves cattle and raised corn, beans and other vegetables for themselves. Before the blight they had gathered chestnuts and sold them. Now they sometimes sold cabbage and potatoes, and most of them raised chickens and a few hogs. The mountain homes typically were of logs, though often covered by weatherboards. The children usually slept in a "loft" upstairs.

"I believe it was 1930 when the drought hit," Christine said, "and the people — who hadn't been well off before — began having a really hard time. Mr. Hoover gave me money to buy things for them — shoes and overshoes for the children, hose for the girls, mufflers, gloves — also food like flour and sugar. Most of this purchasing program was repeated each year afterward while Mr. Hoover was in office." Files in the Hoover Presidential Library disclose that 33 barrels of flour were trucked to the Rapidan in December 1930. The *Eagle* reveals that E. E. Chapman, Hoover's friend at Criglersville, distributed the flour and other substantial gifts to heads of families that Christmas, and that PFC Lantz of the Marine Camp acted as Santa Claus at the school, distributing clothing, candies and toys to the children.

"I remember taking children to Washington on several occasions," Christine said. "We always had lunch at the White House. Once I had taken a group into a ten-cent store and they saw so many things they wanted we fell behind schedule. I hailed a taxi, and we loaded it up with packages and ourselves. When the driver asked me where to, I said, 'The White House.' He looked at me, at all the packages and at the mountain children. 'Did I hear you right, lady? Did you really say the White House?'"

Asked about supervision of her work, Christine said the Hoovers did not neglect her, though they seldom observed classwork in progress. "An educator named Ray Lyman Wilbur who had been president of Stanford, though he was only Secretary of the Interior then, observed more frequently. And there was a Berea College trustee who was also a New York *Times* editor, who came in his high silk hat and a morning coat. Will Durant visited once — and autographed one of his recently published books for the school, *The Story of Philosophy*..."

Enrollment held between twenty and thirty during Christine's four school years. On January 1, 1933, after Franklin D. Roosevelt had won the election, the Virginia conservation commission took over from Hoover the expense of operating the school, including the teacher's salary (of $125 a month!) until such time as the regular public school system adopted its new budgets. There were additional teachers, including Lucy Yowell (who married Hoy R. Faulk, chief cook at the Marine Camp). She taught mountain children in the mornings, mountain adults in the afternoons, and in the evenings "boys" from nearby Civilian Conservation Corps camps "who had not previously learned to read and write." But enrollment dwindled during the last half of the 1930s as families moved from the park. Ultimately, the building was dismantled, transported up the mountain to Big Meadows and re-erected there as a ranger station and residence.

Christine Vest and Lou Witcofski were married on March 22, 1933. "The children knew I was going to China where Lou was being assigned," she said, "and for days after the wedding they kept asking me questions about that country. I pointed it out to them on the school globe. I was unable to answer all their questions, but it was a pleasure to see how keen their curiosity had become about places beyond the range of their own restricted lives."

She had worked to prepare them for living in the modern world, and she felt that gains had been made, not only through the classes but through the special work with the girls and the parents. The oddities of dress and manners had largely disap-

Captain and Mrs. Lou K. Witcofski in the 1960's remembering when she was the teacher at Hoover School.

peared, and most of the people had lost their fear and suspicion of strangers and knew how to earn and take care of money, which had not been a prominent factor in their former way of life.

"On the whole," she said, "I think the effort paid off. At least one of the boys has become a successful farmer on the level land. One is an apple orchard owner-operator. Others have moved quite far away and, from what I can learn, are successful in their jobs, their marriages, and their community life. Many children of my students have completed college."

The Witcofskis, back from the Orient, visited the Rapidan in 1938. "All the people except the Meadows family were gone and cabins burned and grass and flowers grown over the sites," Christine said. The Witcofskis continue to visit Camp Hoover and vicinity at intervals, from their home in southeastern Virginia, enjoying the increasing glories of nature and remembering the Rapidan past.

VI

Strength of Earth

"President Hoover was like a new man when he reached camp," Admiral Boone said, recalling Rapidan weekends. "He was often very tired when we left Washington. Being a person of the most stern conscience, he never spared himself, and when the depression was added on top of all the other problems, he worked even longer hours and slept less. But his fatigue would start leaving him after he had crossed the Potomac.

"I never saw him happier than when he was on the Rapidan. He could hardly wait to leave the car. He would go put on his rubber boots and hurry out to fish, seldom taking time to change from whatever he had been wearing — often a suit, high white collar and tie, Panama hat. I never saw him in a camp outfit, though I know he had one."

Hoover engaged in "the silent sport" on the Rapidan.
(Herbert Hoover Presidential Library)

Dr. Boone (who had been a personal physician also to Presidents Harding and Coolidge) has returned to the Rapidan several times in recent years, combining nostalgic pleasure with the rendering of valuable aid in the National Park Service project of Camp Hoover preservation. Boone rarely was very far from President Hoover during the four-year Presidential term. He advised the President as to reducing caloric intake which involved curbing a fondness for rich foods and sizable portions. Following assumption of the Presidency, weight was gradually reduced and the lower weight maintained. Boone also shared responsibility for the regimen of outdoor exercise, including more Rapidan weekends than Hoover's conscience might have allowed him had he not been kept convinced they

The coordinating station—called "Duty Shack" or "Box" by the Marines—was not far from the President's cabin. (NPS)

added to his capacity for service.

The President's health was generally excellent — Boone never knew him to stay in bed a day. "But often he had been under pressure until he was near the point of exhaustion. And all too frequently when we reached camp a Secret Service man would come out from the 'box' and tell Richey to call the White House at once. In some periods there was one crisis after another, and sometimes the President would decide to turn right around and go back to Washington. We could see the extraordinary dedication prompting such decisions — and feel his disappointment at being unable to stay for the relaxation he required."

One way or another, however, the President obtained

The Hoovers enjoy the flower-filled grounds. (Library of Congress)

enough rest to keep going. At camp his recuperation was amazingly rapid, and after brief fishing or sometimes a nap or a walk in the invigorating air he would plunge with new energy into urgent work. He was a self-disciplinarian with remarkable ability to keep many projects moving, to make maximum use of time. "I never saw him play cards at camp, or work on jigsaw puzzles which were popular there," Boone said, "or pitch horseshoes. The time he actually spent fishing was small, but he was a master of that art — fastest wrist I ever saw."

The President rose early at camp (as elsewhere), showered and shaved, read the newspapers. "He practically absorbed the papers," Boone said, "— even the sports pages. He had followed sports ever since his years at Stanford — was like a boy in relation to sports. But he read the other news too — almost everything." Breakfast was at about 8 o'clock for the Hoovers and their closest associates. The President did not hike except as required to fish. He did not often ride horseback but did enjoy motoring. Lunch was sometimes carried on automobile trips, sometimes eaten outside at camp.

The President might take a nap in the afternoon, or read. "Westerns or detective yarns when he was very tired, otherwise more serious materials, often related to his responsibilities," Boone said. He read very fast and was considered to have a computer-type mind, retaining and sorting everything ready for use, seldom requiring notes or having others keep records of important discussions. He might recess a conference, go off fishing by himself for a short while, then get going again with the conference, usually having worked out some key problem. Dinner would be around 6:30 or 7, followed by conversations or reading around the open fires. About 10 o'clock the Hoovers would say good-night, perhaps for a time of family talk or of reading before sleep.

Radios were seldom turned on, either by the camp regulars or the guests. "The loveliness of the place captivated people," Boone said, "though thy had their different ways of enjoying it." Sometimes the President would sit quietly for many minutes, smoking his pipe, listening to the stream or the fire or people talking. "He didn't move in on conversation aggressively," Boone said, "but would participate passively, thinking about what was being discussed. If those present showed they wanted to hear him, however, he would talk entertainingly on almost any subject."

Top-notch minds were around him most of the time. Among guests who came most often were Secretary Wilbur and Mrs. Wilbur, Secretary Hyde, Attorney General and Mrs. Mitchell, Patrick J. Hurley who became Secretary of War, other cabinet members, usually one or two at a time, Justice

An outdoor meal for visiting dignitaries. (Herbert Hoover Presidential Library)

and Mrs. Stone, the Mark Sullivans, Col. Lindbergh and his wife Anne, the Lewis Strausses, and many others from government and civilian pursuits. Lindbergh contributed a parchment map-lampshade showing his pioneering flights, which was used in the camp's Town Hall. Admiral Strauss had been Hoover's secretary in the U. S. Food Administration and remained a close friend.

The Lindbergh lamp, with maps of his famous flights, on the lamp shade, was used in Town Hall. (Adm. Joel T. Boone)

Noted writers were sometimes among the guests, though most newsmen stayed at Skyland, Criglersville or Madison, all seeking information about the President's doings and occasionally being admitted to camp. In the summer of 1932 Hoover invited all newsmen assigned to cover the Presidency to be his guests at Rapidan for one day. He showed them around the camp and talked with them freely on almost all subjects.

A list of Rapidan guests during Hoover's term would contain thousands of names, though the often-quoted figure of 9,769 actually included White House guests, not camp guests alone. Perhaps even more remarkable than the total number is the fact that camp guests represented all facets of American life and the further fact that, whether eminent or obscure, they came away with lasting memories of warm hospitality and worthwhile experience. The Hoovers in person belied the widespread impression they were cool and distant. They were, on the contrary, deeply fond of people and unusually pleasant to be near.

School teacher Christine was frequently invited to the camp or to go on rides with Mrs. Hoover. One dinner invitation, issued by Hoover himself through a Marine officer, was delayed in reaching her and a visiting friend. The two young ladies had been out riding, and when they returned to the school they ate a big dinner. Only as they were finishing dessert did the officer reach them by phone. He said he was coming immediately to bring them for dinner with the Hoovers.

"But we've *had* dinner," Christine said.

The officer, however, was in no position to take a negative answer. Barely in time he delivered them at camp. They did their uncomfortable best to act the hungry guests and believed they might have succeeded. But after they had said how much they enjoyed the evening, Major Long came out the door after them and demanded an explanation of their poor appetites. Anxious not to cause trouble for the inviting officer, they evaded. But Long had the advantage, being the one responsible for their transportation back to the school house — a responsibility he adamantly refused to exercise unless they explained.

When they did, he grinned. He took them back inside and told Hoover they had had two dinners. Hoover chuckled with even more than his normal cordiality and confessed the same thing had happened to him once when he was Secretary of Commerce. He had invited two men and their wives to dinner and neglected to inform Mrs. Hoover. He had eaten an early dinner at his club, and Mrs. Hoover had been on a Girl Scout trip and had eaten. Having arrived home about the same time, they were upstairs talking when the door bell rang. The butler answered the door and asked the guests in. Mr. Hoover recognized their voices and explained to Mrs. Hoover what had happened. Quickly he came downstairs to greet the guests, while Mrs. Hoover hurried down the back stairs to alert the servants. Soon Mr. and Mrs. Hoover began their second dinner of the evening with hot consomme, followed by appropriate courses, eating along with their guests despite lack of appetite.

Though overstuffed, Christine and her friend, now, really had enjoyed the evening.

Virginians continued their keen interest in Camp Hoover. The inland fisheries commission searched state law for a legal way to extend the trout-fishing season for the President, but succeeded only in confirming that it was set by the legislature as April 1 to June 30, inclusive, subject to shortening but never lengthening by the commission. This sad fact was transmitted to Carson, who wrote Richey, who told Hoover. But there were two "consolations": (1) The commission called attention to existence of bass in the Rapidan — "and the open season for bass extends from July 1 until the following March 15, so there is no reason why President Hoover should not fish for bass and other species, and if he catches trout in doing so, he would, of course, do as other fishermen do, viz., return them to the water." (2) "It is believed the 1930 legislature will confer upon our commission the power to control the open season in all streams which are adequately restocked, in which event it would be a simple matter to provide an appropriate season for trout in the Rapidan River."

There could be little question the Rapidan was being "adequately stocked" — with Virginia trout and also with Federal trout (sent partly from New Hampshire). Moreover, the fisheries commission, prodded by Carson, was considering in late 1929 construction of rearing ponds on the Rapidan with a capacity of 100,000 fingerlings.

Rustic bridge across Laurel Prong. (Adm. Joel T. Boone)

Long before trout time in 1930 the legislature acted as expected and the commission found itself "in a position to provide such a season for trout fishing on the Rapidan as the President may desire." This new situation satisfied Hoover — but apparently not Madison County. Senator Early and Delegate Porter were energetically pushing bills "to give President Hoover and his guests the right to fish *all year-round* in streams adjacent to the summer White House."

With the approach of spring 1930 the *Eagle* resumed its camp reports, weaving voluminous details around this series of highlights:

February 21 - Hoover plans to use the camp more than last year. Lt. Bell's company of Marines is scheduled to arrive March 5.

March 21 - Hoover plans more office space at camp.

April 4 - Hoover is in Madison County on his first visit of the spring today (a Friday!), accompanied by Secretaries Wilbur and Lamont, Atty. Gen. Mitchell, and Rep. Fort. No ladies this time.

April 11 - Hoover caught nine trout before dinner last Friday. He visited his Mountain School on Saturday, then had time for more fishing... Senator Swanson proposes a scroll to be hung at camp: "Lord, suffer me to catch so large a fish that even in talking of it afterward I shall have no need to lie."

May 2 - A new series of cabins — this one for the Cabinet — is being pioneered by Wilbur, Hyde and Mitchell about two miles below the President's Camp.

May 23 - Most distinguished party at camp since Premier MacDonald's visit — Secretary Stimson, Atty. Gen. Mitchell, two Senators, two Congressmen, also Theodore Roosevelt who is Governor of Puerto Rico.

July 11 - Hoover goes over into Page County for bass fishing, to a location recommended by Rep. J. A. Garber.

This series of news items saw the camp's second season well along before local-interest events ceased or were smothered in an intensification of national and world problems. But very early in 1931 the *Eagle* eye caught signs of new, locally important doings related to Camp Hoover:

January 23 - Engineer Keil and party of five are surveying a route upward from the Marine Camp past Hoover School, to be built by the federal government on new alignment not to exceed 6% grade.

January 31 - Survey is for "Hoover Highway" from Rapidan to Skyland, Stony Man and Marys Rock — 24 miles long — appropriation included in the recent $45,000,000 bill passed as a relief measure.

March 20 - Twenty-seven Marines are readying camp for President and guests. Maj. Long will dam Laurel Prong and pipe to reservoir as the mountain spring is weakened by drought and water is scarce for domestic purposes...

In the wake of Marines comes Mrs. Hoover with guests. Six horses hurriedly sent out from Washington. Plans thrown awry, however, by ten-inch snowfall. Mrs. Hoover and guests have to stay in the Cabinet Camp two miles below the President's.

April 17 - Hoover expected for his first weekend of the year.

May 29 - Hoover and party held up by bad storm near Peola Mills, violent wind bringing cars to standstill. It was night when they reached camp — but in time for the President to broadcast an address to centennial exercises at Cornell University on country-wide hook-up. Fortunately, the phone lines withstood winds of hurricane force which blew small buildings off foundations, uprooted trees and leveled fences.

July 24 - Dr. J. N. Clore presided at Skyline Drive luncheon Saturday at Skyland preceding the turning of first shovelful of dirt on the big project. In presenting Hon. William E. Carson, Dr. Clore extolled him for great park work and bringing President Hoover to Madison County...

Exhibited at this luncheon was a 32-page booklet entitled "The President's Camp on the Rapidan," which the conservation commission had just published to honor Hoover and to promote Shenandoah National Park. It was printed on ivory-colored paper and decorated with artistic maps and sketches of Camp Hoover scenes. The text by Thomas Lomax Hunter briefly introduced the camp and the scenery of the park, then presented at length the historical background of the lands between Washington and the Blue Ridge. It touched upon the virtues of fishing, mentioned the Hoover-MacDonald talks in the interests of world peace, and concluded with these words: "May we hope that the peace born and brooded in these noble hills will grow, like the Rapidan, into a mighty stream and flow down through history a splendid and triumphant tide." This attractive booklet was widely distributed and has now become a collector's item.

As soon as the dirt road (now a park fire road) was completed via Hoover School to Big Meadows, and some sections of Skyline Drive were graded to passability, Hoover began exploring by car where Mrs. Hoover and many guests had previously explored on horseback. He especially liked Naked Creek Overlook, two miles south of Big Meadows, from which the view stretches along the Blue Ridge into the far southern section of the park as well as westward over side ridges into Shenandoah Valley and across to Massanutten Mountain and Allegheny ranges beyond.

The government at first controlled only the right of way for Skyline Drive and had to maintain locked gates at property lines to keep privately owned livestock from straying through fences. Gatemen were present during working hours to pass authorized persons (Richey's permit from the responsible engineer, which is on record, covering all who might be with him or to whom he might issue passes). Frank H. Kiblinger, at the gate above Camp Hoover, remembers waiting once far beyond quitting time for the Presidential party to return. He finally concluded the White House cars had gone off the mountain by another route so he locked the gate and went home. Secret Service men broke the lock and the next day turned it in to authorities with a report. The result? Hoover and Kiblinger became friends and even exchanged occasional correspondence long after Hoover's presidency.

Kiblinger caught the Hoover habit of keeping everything as natural as possible. Soon put in charge of work crews, he never allowed tools or anything artificial to be left over a weekend along a road or trail where the Hoovers might see them. One crew learned the lesson so well, he said, that when a truck accidentally knocked a piece of bark off a tree, they picked the piece up and glued it so perfectly into the hole with sticky sap the injury could not be seen. Kiblinger became one of Mrs. Hoover's volunteer helpers plant-wise, and files from the White House contain correspondence with him about sprouts of a scarce tree which she wanted to start at camp.

Once Kiblinger was riding with men who had a pint of moonshine in their car. By mistake they drove out of a side road between the President's car and that of the Secret Service. Finding themselves where they should never be, subject to suspicion including intent to do violence, they watched for the right combination of curving road and screening vegetation and surreptitiously tossed the bottle into the bushes. They were not stopped. "But no sane person would risk being caught with moonshine by President Hoover!" Kiblinger said.

"I wasn't directly involved in the worst incident," he continued, "—one that really could have activated the Secret Service with the Marines backing them up. A road crew working

Sun porch of President's cabin was used as a study. (Adm. Joel T. Boone)

near Camp Hoover set off a dynamite blast while Mrs. Hoover was on the phone to Washington, and it broke the very wire she was talking over! The reprimand that came down on that one was from pretty high up, and somehow the crew managed to finish their grading without using any more dynamite while the Hoovers were at camp."

The pressure on Hoover went on increasing. Many of his associates kept feeling he could stand no more, perhaps partly because they could not, but always he drew upon reserves no one had known he had. One measure of the load was use of the telephone. In a typical Coolidge year Presidential phone calls averaged about 12,000 a month, but by 1932 the comparable figure for Hoover had reached 42,000 — an average of nearly 150 a day!

The direct line between Washington and the Rapidan functioned all too well. In helping to battle the worldwide depression, as well as in strengthening peace, Hoover had stepped up efficiency through international telephoning — conference calls involving American representatives overseas as well as State Department executives in Washington. When he was at camp the Secretary of State usually did the talking in Washington, but Hoover had previously coached his spokesman and almost invariably listened in on the camp phone, then helped the Secretary digest whatever had been presented from abroad.

During May and June 1931, Germany was near financial

Hoover about to board the Presidential limousine after attending church service in the Recreation Hall at Marine Camp. (Capt. Lou K. Witcofski)

collapse, and the rest of Europe was also on the brink, likely to pull America after it into darker depths of depression. Trying to save the situation, Hoover added to his already heavy workload the planning and arranging of a moratorium on intergovernmental payments, including especially German reparations and other war debts. While the public thought he was fishing, he was working, often by phone, to build enough support to make this bold but necessary step politically and diplomatically feasible. Intimates saw how the strain was adding up and urged him to cancel long-standing speaking engagements in Ohio and Illinois, but he felt cancellation would damage public confidence and thereby worsen the depression. Moratorium negotiations became crucial the weekend before the speaking trip, but this time he stayed at camp putting in long sessions, both on guiding the negotiations and in perfecting the speeches he was to make. He had no time to return to Washington, so he boarded his special train at Orange, not far from the Rapidan.

When this particular crisis was believed to be over, he took a number of those who had also been deeply involved to camp with him, this time expecting actually to rest. But a new development, centering in France, caused him (in the words of the *Eagle's* July 10 issue) "to leave for D.C. post haste, not even waiting for dinner which was almost ready. He had a car follow with sandwiches. The run was made in two hours... Because news of his hasty departure leaked, there was a shake-up in his Secret Service squad."

Times came when the only relaxation was while driving to the Rapidan, certainly not while there unless beyond the reach of the demanding phone. The exact routes varied, partly for security reasons, partly for diverse scenery. But always they climbed gradually up the Piedmont Plateau through fields interspersed with woodlands. Traffic was generally slight, the few towns small and everywhere were connections with United States history — battlefields of the Civil War, Bull Run or Manassas, The Wilderness and Fredericksburg; homes of long-ago Presidents, George Washington down the Potomac a few miles, James Madison for whom Madison County was named, Jefferson and Monroe not many miles south of the camp; while just across the Blue Ridge was the birthplace of Woodrow Wilson. George Washington had been a surveyor on wide reaches of this land and not so very far away had accepted the surrender of Cornwallis which consummated the American Revolution. Such history had been among Hoover's favorite reading as far back as his boyhood in Iowa and Oregon. Richey, aided by Carson, gathered facts about places to visit, and occasionally there were brief contacts with the past as Hoover traveled to or from the Rapidan, seeking strength to solve the problems of the present.

But even the few hours of these drives were often scheduled for discussions — with a cabinet member, say, or someone else who could help fight the depression or solve other world-entwined American puzzles. Hoover often accomplished most in quiet conversations, and small but significant conferences became more and more the Rapidan rule, perhaps too frequently hidden under fictitious reports the President was fishing. When the conferences had not already opened in the car, they started early Saturday afternoon at camp and continued into

113

the night with only a short interruption for dinner. Recesses for fishing became rarer. Sometimes the attacks on urgent problems would have to continue on Sunday, even en route back to Washington on Sunday afternoon.

One of the discussion-action streams flowing and developing through the Rapidan was aviation. Col. Lindbergh and other aviation figures were not guests for their health or pleasure primarily, nor to build boulder dams for trout. Hoover had been influencing aviation since 1924 when, as Secretary of Commerce, he had launched a program to help this infant industry catch up with and surpass its European counterpart commercially, while also becoming a reservoir of personnel and manufacturing capacity to bolster military aviation if necessary. Before he became President the daily mileage being flown in America had already advanced beyond that in all of Europe. There were over a hundred American plants making airplanes, and airways had been marked and lighted between population centers.

One of the dining tables in Mess Hall. (Adm. Joel T. Boone)

The industry had grown so fast, in fact, as to create confusion within itself and in relation to the public. The eager chaos needed to be shaped into a system of airlines regulated to render maximum service. Early Rapidan conferences reached toward this goal and brought congressional action setting maximum charges for carrying air mail, requiring mail planes also to carry passengers, and authorizing the Postmaster General to consolidate or extend routes. Again and again — as in August 1930 with Lindbergh, Warren Irvin Glover of the Post Office Department, Clarence Young of Commerce, Trubee Davison of War, and David Ingalls of Navy — Rapidan conferences worked out further encouragements for aviation. The daily plane dropping Presidential mail was an appropriate accompaniment.

Perhaps even better suited to the camp-conference technique — and to the Chief who had recently headed National Parks Association — was natural-resource conservation. The Rapidan atmosphere personalized by the Hoovers' respect for nature worked its charm toward saving the scenic values of Niagara Falls (treaty with Canada approved by the Senate in 1930); tightening control of oil leases on public lands; providing for wiser use of water for power, irrigation and navigation; reducing overgrazing on western ranges; reclaiming wastelands; planning the great St. Lawrence waterway (treaty with Canada signed in 1932); protecting dwindling forests (2¼ million acres added to the national system); launching the Hoover Dam project on the Colorado River; and, perhaps most appropriate of all, effecting a 40% increase in the national park system, including addition of Carlsbad Caverns, Canyon de Chelly, Death Valley, the Great Smoky Mountains — and Shenandoah National Park.

But the Great Depression snatched Presidential priority early in the Hoover years. History as recently re-assessed — no longer hampered by blinding emotional involvement — demonstrates that many of the most solidly effective moves against the depression were started by Hoover. The RFC (Reconstruction Finance Corporation) was largely shaped by Rapidan conferences so as to make loans, not otherwise available, to strengthen the economic system. Even after the RFC was launched, camp conferences continued to sharpen its effectiveness. Stream-side sessions with the governmental corporation's directors in June 1932, for example, came up with these findings and conclusions:

> More than 95% of money loaned to banks thus far has gone to cities with less than one million in population... 125 closed banks have either been re-opened or their depositors fully paid... Bank failures are down to a near-normal rate from the dangerous rate of nearly 100 a week... More than 250 building and loan associations have been helped so as to avoid foreclosures of mortgages... An amount of $68,000,000 has

already been loaned directly to farmers, $170,000,000 to rail-roads, and so on... A total of $30,000,000 has already been repaid by borrowers...

However, immediate further steps are needed, including a system of Home Loan Discount Banks to protect homes from foreclosure and stimulate construction ... joint committees of industry and finance across the country to help coordinate credit facilities now available, with the RFC's work ... authority to use up to $3 billion for buying bonds of political subdivisions or public bodies, thus providing funds to start construction of income-producing and self-liquidating projects that will increase employment, to make loans upon agricultural commodities, thus steadying price levels, to help the Federal Farm Board extend loans to farm cooperatives and loans for agricultural exports, and to furnish up to $300 million to states in distress and unable to finance themselves... Another conclusion: Federal expenditures must be held within tax income...

All these matters blended into Camp Hoover's historic atmosphere, and it was at the Rapidan's headwaters too that the President faced other crises which could not be revealed at the time without sapping public confidence. Here, Gen. Dawes confided he would have to resign as RFC chairman because his large Chicago bank was weakening toward disaster which could

Newsmen on tour of Camp Hoover. (Herbert Hoover Presidential Library)

start chain-reaction destruction of financial institutions across the country. Former Senator Atlee Pomerene of Ohio (a Democrat) was "smuggled" into the Rapidan for a talk with Hoover that concluded with his agreement to accept the RFC chairmanship, the announcement to come at whatever time the President considered most strategic in strengthening citizen-psychology against panic. And it was at Rapidan that Hoover spent all Saturday night, June 27, 1932, all of Sunday and on until 3 a.m. Monday at the telephone, going without sleep to cope with the worst banking crisis that had yet threatened. With this almost superhuman effort he arranged a combination of RFC and inter-bank loans totalling $80,000,000 which stopped the run on endangered banks. His associates, asked during that time by suspicious reporters what the President was doing, answered in daylight that he was fishing, in darkness that he was resting.

As pressures continued to mount — and criticism to grow despite heroic and largely unpublicized battles to beat the depression — people around the President developed a desire to protect him — at least from unkind words that could not in any way be interpreted as constructive. It was said that sometimes when he succumbed at last to urgings to try again for rest on the Rapidan, he was so exhausted every bone in his body, including his skull, ached. He was advised to take only his family and his physician with him to camp while under much strain, but he would never agree. Mrs. Hoover understood and supported his wish always to have guests there, if not to help him relax, to help solve the nation's problems. He did, as he himself had said, need to escape "the pneumatic hammer of constant personal contacts," but an hour alone would suffice, when urgently necessary, for him to draw quick inspiration and strength from the moving waters and the natural earth, supplementing that which nearly always came to him from people.

At the height of the "protective" time, during the election contest with Franklin D. Roosevelt, there were efforts (noted by Abernethy of the Marines) to keep especially abusive newspapers from reaching the President. "Richey and other secretaries," Abernethy said, "would pick up the papers at the 'duty shack' immediately after the morning mail drop and quickly go through them, pulling out those that were too 'rough'. But the Chief suspected the scheme."

One of Abernethy's assignments was to safety-test, early each morning, the chlorinated water that served the President's bathroom. The Chief, still in bed, or at least in his bedroom, would hear the Marine taking the water samples and call out, "What are the headlines today, Abernethy?"

And Abernethy would answer as casually and innocently as he could. "I don't know, sir. I haven't had time to look at the papers yet this morning."

But despite insurmountable difficulties and severe fatigue, there is now general agreement that Hoover maintained his splendid energies, his grasp of vast patterns of fact, his firmly balanced judgment, and his quiet sense of humor throughout his term of office. Even after his overwhelming defeat by FDR he was well able to chuckle over this depression joke which was circulating among members of his cabinet:

Porch of Town Hall during Hoover occupancy. (Adm. Joel T. Boone)

A banker who had lost his shirt applied for a job with a circus. The circus manager said he couldn't even feed his present employees and had had to kill the lion to feed the tigers.

A keeper chose that moment to announce the gorilla had just died of starvation. Whereupon the banker's enterprising spirit revived and prompted him to propose that they skin the gorilla and put him into the skin, letting him perform in exchange for a square meal — and, of course, a share of the admission-ticket receipts.

The manager agreed, but while the hairily disguised banker was performing in his cage, the lion pulled open a gate and fiercely charged him. The gorilla cried, "Help! Help!" Whereupon the lion whispered, "Shut up, you fool! You're not the only banker out of a job!"

It is even said that Hoover was able to chuckle a second time when Secretary Wilbur commented that the New Deal would quickly end all such troubles by appropriating a hundred or so million dollars to subsidize circuses.

VII

A Place to Remember

On Herbert Hoover's 90th birthday — more than a third of a century after he had received an opossum from a Blue Ridge boy, twenty years after the death of his wife who had been his most constant companion — he received congratulations from around the world. Formal felicitations were tendered by Congress and by the President (the fifth occupant of that office since his own term). Newspapers, including many which had criticized him bitterly during the Great Depression, now praised his achievements (from engineering to statesmanship to literature), his love of mankind and of the natural earth (including trout streams), his sense of humor, his unfaltering integrity. It was remembered that his favorite testimonial was from a boys club and declared simply, "Herbert Hoover is a good egg."

The Hoover sequence of 1964 could be called ideal — understanding and appreciation — then, a little over two months later, on October 20, death. He had been the second oldest ex-President in American history. All flags on Federal buildings, Navy vessels at sea and embassies abroad were flown at half-staff for thirty days of mourning. Tributes were in print and on the air throughout the family of man, including one by Henry J. Taylor which summarized:

Hemlock tree still grows through the Presidential porch. (NPS)

Mr. Hoover saw mankind not as fated, but as struggling. And in spite of the agonies he saw everywhere, he never surrendered the fundamental hope and effort that guided his entire life: That the people of the world could live together in a smaller world, at a higher level of prosperity, without wars. The American nation salutes Herbert Hoover as a patriot, the world salutes him as a friend.

Admiral Boone wrote to the superintendent of Shenandoah National Park: "At the invitation of President Hoover's two splendid sons, Herbert and Allan, Mrs. Boone and I attended the church funeral services in New York, then with the family in the Rotunda of the Capitol in Washington, and accompanied the Hoover family to West Branch, Iowa, for the interment... Never in all my long life have I ever attended as impressive a funeral, nor one with greater dignity and deep inspiration... I am gratified indeed that Mr. Hoover will be

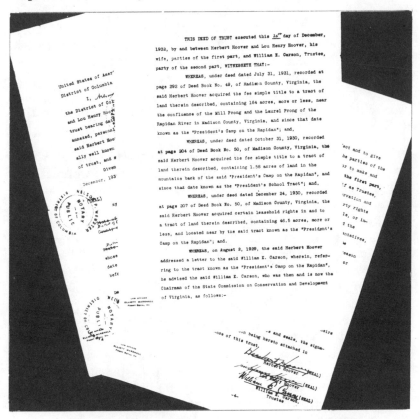

The Hoovers deeded their Rapidan land to be added to Shenandoah National Park (NPS)

121

memorialized by the Rapidan camp which he created and which he and Mrs. Hoover loved so dearly..."

The numerous honors of Hoover's later years could hardly have been predicted on March 4, 1933, when he left the White House and the Rapidan camp to Franklin D. Roosevelt, having received only 59 electoral votes to his opponent's 472. Neither Mr. nor Mrs. Hoover enjoyed the spotlight, and after four years they had continued to shrink from its glare, choosing self-effacement whenever possible. The Hoover performance in the Presidency had been far greater than was yet recognized, though the times had not perfectly matched the dominant Hoover talents which had been, and were yet to be, so tellingly demonstrated.

The pull-out from the Rapidan was little noticed in the storms sweeping the country. Mr. and Mrs. Hoover executed the deed he had promised, turning over to Shenandoah National Park (through William E. Carson, trustee) their ownership of the 164-acre Camp Hoover tract with buildings, the 1.58-acre tract with the Mountain School, and leasehold rights to nearby lands. The Governor of Virginia and many others sent letters of gratitude. Carson arranged to carry out Hoover's desire that the school be continued as long as "necessary, useful and practicable, for the benefit of ·the children residing in the vicinity."

The weather was not right for a farewell visit, and the Hoovers did not come to the camp at the end. He wrote letters of appreciation to those who had helped make the Rapidan community what it had been. Property was inventoried by the Marines, and that belonging to the Hoovers was shipped out. Richey took temporary custody of many items such as fireplace screens, electric refrigerators, hickory chairs and tables, beds, baskets, vases, mirrors. "Old Billy," the President's big horse, went along with the other horses to the Marine base at Quantico. The bachelor officers mess at Quantico received a gift of "three barrels of chinaware and glassware" from the Hoovers.

Abernethy remembers that Mrs. Hoover gave an electric refrigerator to a friend at Madison and many household items to mountain families. Frederick Bates Butler (Brigadier General, U. S. Army, Retired, then a lieutenant in the Corps of Engineers, assigned as assistant director of public buildings and parks, whose concerns in line of duty included such items as furniture) wrote recently: "General Long and I both agree that

The sun porch study as furnished in the 1962 restoration. (NPS)

the only items shipped out of the Rapidan were those owned personally by the Hoovers. As I recall, I arranged to have many of these articles stored temporarily in the Washington Navy Yard pending such time as the Hoovers determined final disposition." Gen. Butler's wife Philippi, then a Hoover secretary, has supplied these further details: "The Hoovers had bought a great deal of furniture themselves for the camp — of appropriate simple style. Some of the Navajo rugs were gifts to Mrs. Hoover from various friends. Also the White House contained a great deal of personal Hoover furniture, books, decorative objects, and so forth. When Mr. Hoover was leaving the Presidency and packing of personal property was in process, great care was taken that no government possessions were included, either from the White House or the Camp."

Thus the Camp remained ready — with basic kitchen and dining equipment from the *Mayflower* and basic furniture made by the Marines — for Hoover's successor.

With the Chief gone, the Marines went on a trout spree. Abernethy said he caught a string of "big ones" and arranged for them to be fried by a Marine cook who was a gourmet specialist with fish. When they came from the kitchen, "they looked beautiful — but tasted horrible, which I guessed was how we felt about the Hoovers leaving... But we found out afterward the cook had fried them in linseed oil, thinking it was Wesson."

The Hoovers left Washington by train immediately after the Roosevelt inauguration, Mrs. Hoover and Allan transferring at Philadelphia to head westward. Hoover and Herbert Jr. went on to New York for necessary business prior to recombining the family at the long-time home on the Stanford University Campus, in California. This home, later given by the Hoover family to the University, became the residence of the institution's president.

The Witcofskis visited the Hoovers in California in the summer of 1933. At lunch, Mr. Hoover asked, "Christine, did you ever have any Rapidan trout up at school?"

She recalled finding fresh trout left at night outside her kitchen door by unknown donors, and she replied, "Mr. President, you wouldn't want me to tell a lie, would you?"

He dismissed the subject with one of his friendly chuckles.

When the accounts were added up, Hoover found he had spent $114,000 in personal funds on the Rapidan development — camp buildings about $50,000; school building, furnishings and operations $12,000; the remainder on 75 miles of trails. In addition, certain operational costs involved large amounts — for example, bills for electricity during full utilization of the camp approached $2,000 a month. Ownership was taken over by the national park without actual legal restrictions, though it is to be noted that, besides the wish (first expressed in a letter to Carson, then repeated in the deed's preamble) that the camp be held available for "my successors," there was an orally expressed hope that, if not used by the President in office, the camp might be available "alternatively to the Boy and Girl Scout organizations." Appraisal commissioners working on condemnation of lands for the park evaluated Hoover's donation at $26,861.80.

An early statement by FDR that he would not use the "summer White House" in Madison, but had men looking in Maryland for a warmer river where he could both fish and swim, was not accepted by Virginia. Carson kept urging a visit, and the new President came with spring. Here, in summary, is the *Eagle's* report of April 14:

> Roosevelt enjoyed his first full holiday since becoming President, driving Sunday in an open touring car through the rolling Virginia country to the Rapidan. A picnic was enjoyed at the camp. With the President were his wife, son John, Mrs. Elliott Roosevelt, Secretary Ickes, Mr. and Mrs. Henry Morgen-

thau, Jr., and half a dozen others. They left the White House about 10:30, gassed up in Criglersville at 1:30, and stayed for more than two hours at the camp. From Rapidan seven cars in the party drove over Skyline Drive to Panorama. Horace M. Albright, director of the National Park Service, accompanied them. At Harrisonburg, Roosevelt spoke enthusiastically to reporters about the park and showed keen interest in plans for its development.

Abernethy and Faulk, two of the Marines left to look after the premises, remember details. Ramps had been prepared over the steps of all camp buildings so Roosevelt could walk into them. When the party arrived, however, Secret Service men picked up the President bodily and carried him to a chair on the porch of Hoover's cabin. He sat there for an hour or more — before, during and after the picnic lunch. Then he was carried back to his car. Faulk (chief cook and commissary steward during the four years he was attached to Radipan, a master sergeant upon retirement) made two trips to Warm Springs, Georgia, with Marines accompanying Roosevelt. He said the ramps remained a long time at Rapidan, until after Roosevelt had adopted "Shangri-La" in Maryland as his principal retreat.

Horace Albright was a member of the Roosevelt party that day. He remembers it was "a gorgeous morning, that Sun-

Navajo rugs again enliven the President's cabin. (NPS)

day morning of April the ninth... But we found out as soon as we got there that the President couldn't handle that, couldn't have stayed around there. It wouldn't be a good place for him... He tried to walk a ways, but he couldn't, so —— I happened to be one of the fellows right near him —— we carried him down to the President's house. Put him on the porch. And later on he went through the place, and he said he thought the terrain was too rough. And I think we all understood that —— although we were disappointed... We talked for an hour. Bill Carson was there, and of course we talked about the park, talked about the road, and Carson insisted that he see the road, the Skyline Drive..."

Kiblinger said that FDR, moving through Big Meadows after leaving Rapidan, was much impressed by the many dead chestnut trees and commented, "It's a 'ghost forest'." That name was used until, quite recently, all but a scattered few of the silvery giants had tumbled to earth.

Roosevelt was at Big Meadows again on July 3, 1936, when he officially dedicated Shenandoah National Park "to the present and succeeding generations of America for the recreation and for the re-creation which we shall find here." Abernethy said the Marines built a rest house for his use on that occasion, "furnishing it with Navajo and other rugs — and tearing it down after the dedication."

While FDR visited Rapidan but once, Abernethy said Mrs. Roosevelt came again — with "a bunch of ladies." During that period, he said, there were frequent parties of Federal officials at Camp Hoover.

The *Eagle* picked up a rumor in April 1933 that Vice President and Mrs. Garner might use the Rapidan. The paper stated the camp could be put back into full operation at little expense. A party headed by House Speaker Rainey appeared shortly thereafter and made an "unofficial inspection" — which kept the entire issue alive, at least in the hopeful minds of Madison.

A movement had meanwhile been set in motion, primarily by Carson but with White House knowledge, to provide at Rapidan a swimming pool for Roosevelt. Maj. Long was involved as were National Park Service engineers and architects. The Virginia conservation commission would furnish supplies and equipment, and the CCC would do the work. Long had made a pencil sketch and the Park Service was drawing up detailed plans and specifications. The U. S. Public Health Service was soon involved. Disagreement developed between the Long group, which wanted a rectangular concrete pool 25 by 70 feet with vertical sides, and Park Service personnel who favored a naturalistic "ole swimmin' hole" with sloping banks.

In June 1933 blueprints were sent by NPS Director Albright to Carson at Richmond. Carson felt the "ole swimmin' hole" might meet the requirements — but first he wanted a dependable estimate of the cost, "as we are very closely run for money and it may be that we cannot go along." An estimate of $5,045 was furnished — main item being $3,000 for an oil-burning plant capable of raising 100,000 gallons of water 25 degrees in twelve hours. A question of whether the concrete might be stained ultramarine blue came briefly to the fore. But on June 28 Carson confessed his commission was unable "at this time" to pay the cost "but hopes to go ahead soon."

The pool project was never revived, but confusion as to Camp Hoover's future continued. The *Eagle* announced on June 30 that T. T. Early had been placed in charge of restoring the camp "to its former beauty" with CCC help. Marines were renewing a contract with Madison Power to supply current. "Several members of the official family have just recently visited the lodge, among them Navy Secretary Swanson who has made several trips." A week later the *Eagle* reported that Early and about "50 CCC young men have completed a new road at the summer White House so autos can drive right up in front of it."

That thread ravelled into nothingness, but in May 1934 the National Park Service was instructed from above to prepare plans for the Rapidan buildings "so that each cabin will be a complete unit for cooking, dining and sleeping." Drawings for eight cabins were transmitted from Shenandoah park headquarters on June 18, with indications additional buildings were being studied. Then this thread disappeared.

On April 24, 1935, Secretary of the Interior Ickes instructed the Park Service: "Necessarily, President Roosevelt is not able to make such use of the camp as President Hoover undoubtedly had in mind. Whether it is to continue to be a Presidential camp must, therefore, be left for future determination." In the meantime it would be all right to permit members of the Cabinet to use the camp. "This use is consistent with Hoover's desire, as Cabinet members used it during his

Fireplace and some of the furniture in the Prime Minister's cabin today. (NPS)

administration." Visitors, but only on permit, may inspect the camp, but "not fish or occupy the buildings." Ickes himself would issue permits to Cabinet members, but the NPS Director could issue the other permits when there was no conflict.

On June 12 Ickes authorized Secretary of the Navy Swanson (former Virginia Governor and U. S. Senator) to use the camp "for an indefinite period"—which cancelled out Park Service plans to host a session of the 15th National Conference of State Parks at Rapidan. The camp continued in a sort of limbo. A study was started in 1936 of the cost of repairing the buildings (beyond what the CCC could do) but was not completed. When Swanson and his wife revealed they would be coming to the camp about July 1 that year, a question was raised as to whether the electrical bill was to be paid from Shenandoah's limited appropriation, or whether the Navy Department might pay it. This question was again raised in 1939 and information given that the bill, paid by the park, had been $357.60 in 1937 and $323.60 in 1938 — and the Swansons were again expected that summer.

Reviewing the Swanson period, Faulk said the Secretary was so ill and old a chief pharmacist's mate always kept watch over him, though Mrs. Swanson was usually with him too. Abernethy said Swanson "loved the park and was very grateful to the Marines for all they did for him, at camp and elsewhere." Swanson once asked, "Are there Marines in Heaven?"

"I doubt it, sir," Abernethy replied.

"Then I don't want to go there."

Swanson died at Camp Hoover on July 7, 1939. All Navy property was then withdrawn, and the National Park Service assumed direct charge, employing a caretaker at $90 a month.

Also during the last half of the thirties the mountain people were being moved out so park land could return to natural conditions. Kiblinger and a helper were once assigned the unpleasant task of burning vacated houses so as to remove temptation to prospective squatters, perhaps the very families that had been resettled. In one house they found a chest of love letters from Marines to girls of this large family. They spent hours with these letters, reconstructing the relationships, wondering how many of the promises had been kept. They could hardly bring themselves to burn a house, tumbledown though it was, which had held so much of human living and longing.

The Slums at Camp Hoover where Secretary of the Navy Swanson died in 1939. (NPS)

The Camp Hoover problem, in some aspects, resembled that of the old mountain homes as time and weather gnawed at structures which had not been built to last forever and were not regularly used or fully maintained. Organizations and individuals had wanted to use it, for one occasion or permanently, ever since the Hoovers had left it — starting with the "Women of the U. S. Naval Reserve Force" and continuing with religious groups, orphans homes, resort businesses, and persons who would buy a cabin and move it away. The camp was a hot-potato puzzle. As long as any possibility remained of its being utilized by Presidents, it could hardly be treated simply as part of the national park used by all citizens equally or repossessed by nature.

In 1941 a plan to utilize the camp for conferences between Interior Department executives and Members of Congress surfaced in the form of instructions to the Shenandoah superintendent that condition of cabins and furniture be checked at once — and the caretaker's wife (if any) asked whether she would serve as a cook. The eleven buildings were reported not in the best of condition, and early next year, having heard no more of the latest plan, the Superintendent recommended that either an appropriation be obtained for repairs or the most dilapidated buildings (the entire Marine Camp and part of Camp Hoover itself) be torn down and hauled away.

Neither alternative was accepted, but a different plan was set in motion — to allow the park concessioner to repair and operate the camp as part of its visitor-accommodation system. Yet after Virginia Sky-Line Co., Inc., had started work the Secretary of the Interior had second thoughts and wrote that, "inasmuch as rubber and gasoline will be so difficult to get" because of war-caused rationing, "it would be well to postpone indefinitely the operation of the Rapidan."

The Marine Camp, which had worked itself out of tents into wooden barracks during the thirties, was demolished with Secretarial approval in 1944, and the caretaker, who had been living there, moved to the Creel in Camp Hoover itself.

In 1946 the park superintendent reported there had been no use of Camp Hoover since 1941 and again posed the alternatives of obtaining adequate funds for repairs or removing the buildings. This time Interior agreed the National Park Service had no legal obligation to keep the buildings but believed Hoover should be consulted before any steps were taken to eliminate them. A letter to Hoover was drafted for the signature of the Secretary, but the insoluble puzzle again caused procrastination, and the letter was never sent. Next year two plans were discussed — regular use by Members of Congress or regular use by Boy and Girl Scouts. An Assistant Secretary came to inspect what was now being called by a leading Washington newspaper the "Rapidan Ghost Town."

National Capital Area Council, Boy Scouts of America,

Hoover revisited his old camp in 1954 while it was serving as a Boy Scout Camp.
(Joseph J. Davis)

was well aware of Hoover's fondness for Scouting, once expressed in these words: "The Boy Scout movement has opened for boys the portals to adventure and constructive joy — by reviving the lore of the frontier and the campfire; by establishing contacts with the birds and sometimes with the bees; by matching their patience to the deliberative character of fish; by efficient operation of the swimming hole; and by peeps into the thousand mysteries of the streams, and the trees, and the stars."

Scout officials contacted the ex-President in New York and received both encouragement and help behind the scenes. A $50,000 grant was offered by the Avalon Foundation (a creation of Mrs. Ailsa Mellon Bruce, daughter of Hoover's Secretary of the Treasury) to put the camp in condition for Scout use. The council pushed negotiations with Interior, and in March 1948 the Secretary informed Hoover the way had been cleared "to make the Rapidan camp facilities available to the Boy Scouts under an appropriate lease ... which will include a provision that these facilities will be released by them if they are again wanted for a Presidential camp." For the record, he pointed out that the plan was "not entirely in keeping with the long-established policies and principles of the National Park Service in not permitting exclusive use of national park lands by any group or interest" — but he declared this to be a special situation.

When the lease to the Boy Scouts was about to be signed, the Girl Scouts became interested. Their Washington camping chairman made a hurried trip to the Rapidan, then said they would like to use the camp "in conjunction with the Boy Scouts." But the girls were too late. The lease was signed for twenty years, the Boy Scout council to have full use of the camp and to be responsible for both maintenance and operation. Access was to be from below, via Criglersville, the fire road from Big Meadows having a locked gate.

The council sent a work party to prepare for all-year use. Toilet fixtures were removed from several cabins and the bathrooms converted into kitchens. Almost immediately there was an emergency, and park rangers spent an anxious four hours searching for lost Scouts who, the camp director later wrote, apologizing, "were a little too enthusiastic about putting their training into practice."

Outlines of the fast-developing, new situation showed in

notes made by the chief ranger while accompanying Scout officials on an inspection tour in March 1949:

> A hundred yards west of old Mess Hall seven tent frames are now in place, rock fireplaces constructed, standard pit toilet built. Twelve trees from 4" up had been felled (!), showing need to make park policies better known. One tent site at old Five Tents, one halfway up road to camp boundary, another at boundary fence...
>
> Engineer of Scout council looks over dam sites for swim pool. I discouraged idea but outcome unknown.
>
> Work had been done — porches removed, partitions changed, stoves and cooking utensils in all the lower cabins including President, Prime Minister and Town Tall. Toilet similar to one at tent site between Slums and Ishbel. Lower boards and rotted sills had been replaced. (Chimney screens needed.) Some small work on power lines and phone line.

Four days in June 1949 brought 15.25 inches of rain and washed out a bridge and 75 feet of road two miles below camp — reminding oldtimers of torrents plaguing that road during first construction twenty years before. Some Scouters began to wonder if the council had not undertaken a bigger task in this wilderness than it could sustain in the long pull. But enthusiasm was high, and the council was able to persuade Army Engineers from Fort Belvoir to replace the bridge and road. Trouble then developed in the phone system, which by this time depended on a battered cable running on the ground to the Hoover School site, 2 miles, thence 1.5 miles to Big Meadows. Road erosion remained a constant threat, and meeting fire-protection standards was repeatedly bothersome and expensive. But the effort continued and a valuable program grew, mostly involving older boys called Explorers.

A publicity flurry in mid-1949 envisioned a combination of Scout camp and historic shrine — enough years having passed, perhaps, for values which had long hovered there to be recognized as historically significant. A committee of Washington civic leaders, including Richey and Mrs. Edwin George Bowman (who had been in charge of Girl Scout Little House), was reported by the New York *Times* to be planning restoration of buildings, especially the President's lodge, and of original furnishings. Approval was widely expressed, but little evidence to support the publicity appeared on the Rapidan.

After the election of 1952 it appeared the Scouts might

have to vacate in favor of the new President. Truman had shown no interest in Camp Hoover, though going occasionally to the tamer Shangri-La in Maryland, but Eisenhower was the kind of fisherman who might enjoy the Rapidan. The Scouts declared Ike could move right in. The National Park Service studied cost of putting the camp once more in Presidential condition, and the Director prepared a report (and welcome) for Eisenhower. But suspenseful months went by without the President's wishes becoming known.

The Scouting program was by now in full bloom. A printed pamphlet, "Camp is Calling!" urged Scouts to make their reservations early for the special July 12-August 8 period:

> Camp Hoover is one of the outstanding Explorer Camps in the country... Nine different sites are available — two basic sites, cleared areas with water, latrine and firewood; three tent sites pre-equipped, with tents on platforms, cots, kitchen and dining shelter, tables, benches, latrine, water and firewood; four cabins, three accommodating 8 persons each, Prime Minister, Ishbel and Trail's End, one called the Mellon Cabin accommodating 24 persons.
>
> Fees for the special summer period $1 per Scout per week at a basic site, $2 per week for an equipped site or cabin... Fees at other times $1 per troop or post per night basic, $2 at equipped site, $4 to $8 per troop or post per night in cabins... Each troop provides and prepares its own meals.
>
> A trained central staff will be available during the special period — expert guides and woodsmen... Trail hikes, outpost camping, campfires, survival hikes, limited sports and swimming and trout fishing are some of the opportunities...
>
> A Junior Leaders' Training Course will be conducted June 20-28... Facilities limit enrollment to 125...

A mimeographed camp guidebook contained additional information on many aspects of location and program:

> This mountain type of hiking is new to most boys and requires conditioning. We suggest a half-day or one-day trip early in the week to try out the strength and skill of the boys — before attempting any of the overnight, three-or four-day hikes...
>
> This year we will "Pack the Trails" for the first time. We have secured four pack burros which will be used for longer trips directly from camp. This will be an experience that boys will long remember...

Nature experiences should play an important part in a Scout's time in camp. But leaders should not despair because they cannot rattle off the names of objects like a professor of taxonomy! Knowledge of species is not half so important as an understanding of broad natural relationship and the ability to pass those ideas and interests on to boys. The camp has a Nature Trail, well marked and loaded with interesting items... We will keep a seasonal bird log, and an all-time bird log; perhaps you and your boys can contribute to the record...

Although the camp has no swimming pool or lake, there are in the streams many small pools which lend themselves to bathing or dipping. Boys will brag afterwards about having "swam" in the coldest water in any camp...

Eisenhower never came to the Rapidan, preferring to fly for fishing in the Rocky Mountains. Scout Executive Andrew J. Murphy reported 282 boys attending the special four-week session in 1953, and 110 leaders at the training conference, these figures doubling the count of previous years. By 1954 the burro trips had become one of the most popular activities, combined with an intensive program on how to handle a burro (saddling, packing and leading). The pack parties were on the trail away from camp for eight meals.

That summer brought an unforgettable event. Herbert Hoover, accompanied by Lawrence Richey, returned to the Rapidan which they had not seen for more than twenty years. The Scouter responsible for the barbecue dinner which marked that occasion, Joseph J. Davis (now Director of Camping, Philmont Scout Ranch and Explorer Base, New Mexico) vividly recalls the ex-President's visit. As the limousine approached the foothills, Hoover said, "Stop the car here. My old friend, the county highway supervisor, lives here." Hoover found his friend ill and bedfast and spent about twenty minutes with him. "What a reunion that must have been," Davis commented, " — the former President of the United States and an unknown county highway supervisor who was his friend."

Among those at the dinner were Delmer H. Wilson, scout executive of the National Capital Area Council (now personnel director, Boy Scouts of America), other Scout leaders and members of the council's executive board, and Superintendent and Mrs. Guy D. Edwards of Shenandoah National Park. The meal was eaten around the massive outdoor fireplace, one of the first structures at Camp Hoover. "I served Mr. Hoover's

Joe Davis serves the ex-President at the memorable
barbecue dinner. (Courtesy Joseph J. Davis)

plate with the steak, chicken and potato and pushed it in front
of him," Joe Davis said. "I was about to remove the foil from
around the potato when he said, 'Hold on! The Governor of
Idaho taught me how to prepare Idaho baked potatoes!' With
that, he took the potato, foil and all, and wrapped his napkin
around it. He carefully kneaded it for about a minute, then he
said, 'There, it's ready to be opened.' I've been preparing baked
potatoes that way ever since."

After dinner Hoover sat at the base of a large hemlock
tree and enjoyd a cigar while conversing. Later he conducted
the group around the camp, telling of events there when he
was President. He gave praise and encouragement to the Scout
leaders — and friendly greetings and handshakes to all Scouts
who were there. Before leaving, he and Richey, at first together, then separating for solitude, walked along the stream and
the old trails, remembering.

The Scout-camp period lasted ten years. The access road
via Criglersville continued to give trouble. For a time park
officials permitted use of the fire-road link with Skyline Drive,
but such favoring of a few (in proportion to the millions of
park visitors) could not become regular policy. Termite damage was found in buildings, and other facilities also deteriorat-
ed. The state health department found water samples contam-

Hoover and party walking trails. (Joseph J. Davis)

inated — immediate solution, boiling; long-range solution, renewing the water system.

Partly because of difficult access and partly, some said, because of lack of a lake for water sports, the number of Scouts using Camp Hoover, though substantial, had not come up to expectations. As of July 1, 1958, after spending on the camp more than $50,000 beyond income, the council regretfully pulled back its strength to where it could serve more boys. The National Park Service resumed direct responsibility, and the camp was once more in limbo, a part of the park yet still to be held for Presidential use which might never materialize.

Cost of maintaining the original buildings would now be very high, and there was the further complication of Scout structures. R. Taylor Hoskins (the park's first chief ranger, a man who had known the camp in its original form) now returned as superintendent. The old alternative of adequate appropriations or demolition confronted him squarely and through him the Department of the Interior. Hoover, now in his mid-eighties, was promptly consulted this time. He named Richey and Boone as his representatives in working out the camp's future.

They conferred with National Park Service officials, and

The Creel was the home of Larry Richey and Joel Boone when they were at camp in the Hoover years. (Adm. Joel T. Boone)

decision was reached to demolish all buildings but three and to rehabilitate and preserve these — The President, The Prime Minister, and Creel — as essential features of a permanent historical-natural shrine. That same year (1959), after spending Chistmas with Hoover in New York, Richey was on a plane bound for Washington. As it was losing altitude for a landing, the stewardess tried to awaken him. But the man who had been identified with Camp Hoover from the site-search on through the many vicissitudes was dead.

Bids were asked on 24 buildings (more than half of them Scout structures·), to be torn down and removed from the site. Highest bid was $331, and they were sold for that amount, most of the lumber being partially decayed or termite-riddled. The grounds were cleared for return of natural conditions, leaving only the three chosen cabins, the outdoor fireplace and Mrs. Hoover's stone fountain.

Shortly after the demolition, in a brief ceremony at Madison on August 17, 1960, Hoover's friend Rear Admiral Lewis L. Strauss presented a bronze tablet to be placed on Madison County's brick courthouse. The *Eagle* reported that Strauss, now a resident of neighboring Culpeper County, was introduced by Carlton Clore who had been a barefoot boy at Madison's "Hoover Day" exactly thirty-one years before. Strauss said the

Herbert Hoover plaque on Madison County Court House (NPS)

tablet carried out Hoover's wish that his gratitude to Madison people find expression. Claude Yowell accepted for the county, reminding listeners of the boost given roads, schools and Madison life in general by Hoover. The words in bronze read:

On August 17, 1929, Herbert Hoover, President of the United States, met with the citizens of Madison County as their neighbor and friend and eloquently thanked them for their hospitality.

Speaking of his fishing camp at the headwaters of the Rapidan River, Mr. Hoover concluded his remarks with these words:

"Next to prayer, fishing is the most ... constant reminder of the democracy of life, of humility and of human frailty –– for all men are equal before fishes. And it is desirable that the President of the United States should be periodically reminded of this fundamental fact — that the forces of nature discriminate for no man."

Generous amounts of care and dedication, plus approximately $28,000, went into rehabilitation work at Camp Hoover from 1960 to 1963. Some of the original furniture was found, renovated and placed in The President and The Prime Minister (Creel being occupied by the caretaker). Massive-posted pine beds, wicker chairs and couch are among such pieces in The President. A mahogany secretary which had been in the living quarters at the Mountain School is one of the pieces in The

Prime Minister.

Admiral Boone was the surviving consultant now, representing the former President, "who, with advancing age, no longer had the strength to leave New York." With Superintendent Hoskins and Park Naturalist E. Ray Schaffner, concerned with restoration and with recording the story, the Admiral and his wife went over the camp in detail on October 24, 1962, providing both facts and feelings:

> The tents, then the first building called Five Tents, were on this slope — jungle land now as when we first came. But here's the big stepping stone used to mount horses, especially by Mrs. Hoover and other ladies. If Mrs. Hoover were alive she could give a living history. She had a great mind, almost equal to President Hoover's. Both loved this place, and the boys also spent considerable periods here. Of course Herbert Jr. was confined to bed here about two months due to illness...
>
> A building there — Major Long and his wife lived in it part of the time... And this one, the Creel, was the last constructed — it consisted of one large combined living and bedroom with an adjacent bathroom when Richey and I occupied it...
>
> President Hoover was a very, very experienced fisherman, but of course he can no longer go up and down stream banks. He got more relaxation from fishing than anything else. It was his great love — to fish as in his childhood... I'll see him next week in New York and tell him about this visit and the progress made.

CAMP HOOVER

A diligent search was begun in 1928 by President Hoover's personal representative, Mr. Larry Richey, for a suitable site for a summer camp for the Chief Executive. He was assisted by William E. Carson of Riverton, Virginia. They chose this site in early 1929 because it met the three guidelines laid down by the President. It is within 100 miles of Washington D.C., situated on a trout stream and is at an elevation of 2,500 feet above sea level so that it is virtually free of mosquitoes.

When Mr. Hoover retired from office, he gave this land for inclusion in Shenandoah National Park.

Informational sign and map now help guide visitors around Camp Hoover. (NPS)

Pictures were secured showing furnishings, and Hoskins (who had been superintendent at Carlsbad Caverns) used his southwestern knowledge to secure Navajo rugs resembling those originally placed by the Hoovers. Two original maps of the camp (and their original frames) were contributed by Mrs. Butler and hung in the President's lodge. A pitcher used there was donated by Mrs. Gertrude Bowman... In 1963 Hoskins reported to Boone: "The historical marker has been completed and erected, and pictures of all buildings with appropriate scripts have been placed in metal frames and mounted in laminated plastic. A wooden map has been erected showing the layout of the camp."

Admiral Boone (left) and Darwin Lambert during one of the interviews which helped produce this book. (E. Ray Schafiner, NPS)

The National Park Service continues to honor Hoover's wishes. The policy statement—approved by the Secretary of the Interior after the Boy Scout period and the rehabilitation and refurnishing of three of the original structures—provides for "making the camp available not only to the President but also the members of his Cabinet. Occasionally it has been available to members of Congress. This has worked very well . . ." Availability is on a first come, first served basis

When not in use under the first Hoover priority, the camp is simply a rather wild part of the Park, not accessible to visitors by automobile. It can be reached by hiking from Byrd Visitor

Center at Big Meadows (round trip about six miles). Sometimes it is the goal of hikes or other excursions conducted by park personnel.

Presidential interest has varied. After finding the camp too rough for him to use, FDR did not return but relaxed mostly at Hyde Park, N. Y., Shangri-La, Md. (later called Camp David), and Warm Springs, Ga. Truman used Shangri-La and the Navy yacht *Williamsburg;* Eisenhower, Camp David and Gettysburg; Kennedy, Hyannis Port; and Johnson, his LBJ Ranch. Nixon expressed such interest in Camp Hoover that a helicopter pad was prepared at Big Meadows to aid his access, but the years went by and he never came. Ford never came either, having a favorite resort in the Colorado Rockies.

Carter was the first President since FDR to visit Camp Hoover. He came briefly on an inspection tour. Later he brought Rosalynn and Amy and enjoyed fishing and relaxing on the Rapidan (May 11-14, 1979). Vice President Mondale enjoyed the camp thoroughly and often, sometimes earlier in spring or later in autumn than the unwinterized facilities had been intended for. A forest-damaging ice storm once caught him at camp. Utilities and communication went out, greatly upsetting the Secret Service. Park personnel had to ''saw in'' to him and saw still more bent or broken trees to bring him out.

Up to the time of this writing (July 1983) Reagan has not come to Camp Hoover, but the camp has been used by many of his close associates at the White House. Recognition of the camp's historical significance and inspirational power has continued to grow. Memories of people who spent time here with the Hoovers still bring strong elements of the meaningful past to life. Captain Witcofski and his wife Christine revisited several years after the rehabilitation, and Christine wrote:

> We watched a bear crossing the road in front of us, and I speculated if that had happened thirty-five years ago just how many, if any, children would have come to school...
>
> After we passed the chain barrier on the road, I was on familiar soil — but, oh, how underbrush can grow...
>
> The camp looked so familiar — but no Marine Major to greet us. I missed Town Hall and the Mess Hall, but the President's ''Brown House'' looked so good and familiar... I stood on the porch remembering things I hadn't thought of since I left there in 1933. The streams looked the same — the hemlocks so

peaceful and the gurgle of the water, all the same...

I entered the President's cabin. It doesn't show age, and the inside was not dark as old woods often are. A number of chairs looked like the originals. Indian rugs were on the wall, but I missed most Mr. Hoover's old felt hat, his fishing gear, Mrs. Hoover's knitting, and in the bedrooms the Indian print bedspreads and bits of Indian pottery, and always the bowls holding colorful branches of leaves, especially the red, red leaves of sumac...

The color map of Camp Hoover, drawn by Edward L. Stone when President Hoover was often here, was presented by Major E. C. Long, USMC, to A. H. Cave, Clerk of Madison County, in December 1932. It was made available for reproduction in this book through the courtesy of Charles J. Ross, a successor of Mr. Cave.

He was proud to the end that a boys' club had formally declared, "Herbert Hoover is a good egg." (Harris & Ewing)